Simone Weil

Twayne's World Authors Series
French Literature

David O'Connell, Editor
University of Illinois

TWAS 723

SIMONE WEIL
(1909–1943)
Photograph courtesy of Simone Pétrement

Simone Weil

By John M. Dunaway

Mercer University

Twayne Publishers • *Boston*

To Denise and Vladimir

Simone Weil

John M. Dunaway

Copyright © 1984 by G. K. Hall & Company
All Rights Reserved
Published by Twayne Publishers
A Division of G. K. Hall & Company
70 Lincoln Street
Boston, Massachusetts 02111

Book Production by Elizabeth Todesco

Book Design by Barbara Anderson

Printed on permanent/durable acid-free
paper and bound in the United States of
America

**Library of Congress Cataloging in
Publication Data**

Dunaway, John M., 1945–
  Simone Weil.

  (Twayne's world authors series; TWAS 723. French
literature)
  Bibliography: p. 131
  Includes index.
  1. Weil, Simone, 1909–1943. I. Title.
II. Series: Twayne's world authors series; TWAS 723.
III. Series: Twayne's world authors series. French literature.
B2430.W474D85 1984   194   84–10842
ISBN 0-8057-6570-0

Contents

About the Author

A native Georgian, John Dunaway received the bachelor's degree from Emory University and the Ph.D. from Duke University in 1972. Since that time he has taught at Mercer University in Macon, Georgia, where he is associate professor of modern foreign languages. He is the author of *The Metamorphoses of the Self: The Mystic, the Sensualist, and the Artist in the Works of Julien Green* (Kentucky, 1978) and *Jacques Maritain* (Twayne, 1978). His work has appeared, among other places, in the *South Atlantic Review,* the *French Review,* the *Review of Politics,* and the University of South Carolina's *French Literature Series.*

Preface

One has, in reading Simone Weil, a whole range of emotional reactions: from skepticism and doubt to admiration and a sense of moral obligation. It is not entirely without reason that her classmates sometimes called her "the categorical imperative in skirts." Often when Weil speaks of what should be done about human needs and suffering, one has an inescapable sense of duty. One feels obliged to admit the necessity of such actions, even though they are usually very demanding. It is because of the deep moral strength in her work that she speaks to our noblest impulses. On the other hand, there is the not infrequent negative response, dictated by common sense, that prompts one to accuse her of having gone too far. It is her strength and her weakness that she does indeed carry some lines of thought to astonishing lengths. Her philosophy and her life were diametrically opposed to the complacency, the acedia, the lukewarm unassertiveness of modern bourgeois ennui. It is in this sense that she offers—both in her life and in her writings—the antidote to the moral sickness of modern man so tellingly diagnosed by Eliot, Baudelaire, and the existentialists.

I first became interested in Weil through conversations with colleagues and friends. As I got more deeply immersed in this project I found that although her name is hardly a household word, those who do know the life and work of Simone Weil are usually very intrigued with, if not devoted to, her ideas.

As a Christian layman (a Protestant with a particular interest in French Catholic writers), I find Weil's religious thought inspiring and illuminating, although at times it appears to be too willingly eclectic. There has been, as one might have expected, a great debate over whether she was ever truly converted to Christianity or to Catholicism. I should like to make it clear from the onset that while I believe her thought often fails to conform to orthodox Christian dogma, I am convinced that her personal religious experience was an authentic and powerful encounter with Jesus Christ. The accounts of her mystical experiences that appear in *Attente de Dieu (Waiting for God,* 1950) and in her letters are unmistakably stamped with the transforming character of Christian commitment.

As a student of French literature and philosophy, I have found Weil's writings to be useful and revealing documents in the history of ideas and in the unique cultural identity of the French people. As a teacher confronted with attempts to redefine the goals and curricular implementations of a liberal education, I have profited immensely from her concept of education, of roots and the crisis of modern culture.

Weil's thought is holistic. Everything connects. There is never a realm of artistic, philosophical, political, or spiritual discourse that is considered separately or autonomously. All the most urgent questions are interrelated for her. This holistic vision is undoubtedly accounted for in large part by her immersion in the masters of classical antiquity, and it is something that needs to be kept in mind as we move from one subject to another. For she herself would want her reader to avoid the compartmentalization of knowledge that has often afflicted modern thought.

The wholeness of Weil's vision has resulted in a unique blend of rigid intellectual discipline and profound human compassion, the latter never tainted by shallow sentimentality and the former saved from dogmatic severity by her passionate thirst for truth. At bottom, one finds that Simone Weil's life and thought are inextricably bound together in the most profound and quintessential motivation of the search for truth. For she included in truth the concepts of beauty, virtue, and goodness.

Father Joseph-Marie Perrin, in attempting to sum up and evaluate the message of Simone Weil, cautions us to distinguish carefully between the wheat and the chaff. "It is necessary, then, to sort out her thoughts in order to know them and the truth of them; it is she herself who invites us to do so."[1] He cites repeated insistences by Weil that it is up to her readers to judge the quality and veracity of her thought: "It is for others to discern the value of this and where it comes from."[2] My own experience with reading and interpreting Weil is that one needs a great deal of wisdom, careful thought, and divine guidance in order to accomplish the "sorting out" task recommended by Perrin. However imperfectly I have succeeded, I encourage the reader to pursue the unfinished work, and to that end I have tried not only to present her most valuable insights but to suggest what appear to me to be weaknesses in her broadly ranging philosophy.

This study is intended only as an introduction to the subject, primarily for the use of the nonspecialist. There is much that could have been developed in more depth, especially in regard to Weil's debt to the Greeks, her critical judgments in aesthetics, and her theories on mathematics and science. I have also chosen not to deal at all with Weil's play *Venise sauvée* (1955) or her poetry, for reasons of space limitations and because this is generally considered a minor and rather weak area in her oeuvre.

Simone Weil bibliography is indeed a confusing maze through which the reader would be able to proceed only with difficulty and by dint of persistence, were there no guideposts along the way. All her books were published posthumously, and most are composed of miscellaneous letters, articles, notes, and fragments, much of which was never intended for publication. The English translations frequently group these materials under different titles. It is because of the haphazard nature in which her works appeared and the holistic connectedness of her thought that Weil's views on a given subject can hardly be traced to a single text. For this reason I have attempted to include certain bibliographical aids in the following form: First, the Selected Bibliography at the end contains under primary sources a parenthetical note for each original edition indicating which translation (or translations) includes the contents for that specific book. Second, in the first end-noted reference to each primary source I have identified the contents and the dates and circumstances in which they were originally written. Finally, a passage in the Conclusion sketches out the critical reception that has greeted Weil's works in France, England, and the United States from 1947 to the present.

The writing of this book was greatly facilitated by the generous support of Mercer University. I am especially grateful for the sabbatical leave that enabled me to travel to France in 1980, where many fruitful contacts were made. I wish to thank Gustave Thibon, Father Joseph-Marie Perrin, Simone Pétrement, André Devaux, Eveline Garnier, Carmen de Zayas, and M. and Mme Robert Gaillardot for giving me such a warm welcome and sharing their invaluable insights into Weil's life and work. I have profited as well from conversations on this project with all of the following: André Weil, Wallace Fowlie, William Bush, Arthur Evans, Father Thomas Healy, Dan Metts, Vincent Leitch, Eliot Youman, Cathy Meeks, Ray Brewster, Eric Springsted, and Diogenes Allen. Dumont Bunn and

Clare Zens were instrumental in obtaining books and articles through interlibrary loan, and Mrs. Angela Snyder typed the first draft of the manuscript. Russell Woodard came to my aid in solving various reference problems, and my editor, David O'Connell, was indeed resourceful and patient in helping me improve my manuscript. As always, I owe my heartfelt gratitude to my wife, Trish, and children, Michael and Jenny, for their patience and moral support. But my deepest thanks go to Denise and Vladimir Volkoff, to whom this book is affectionately dedicated.

John M. Dunaway

Mercer University
February 1983

Chronology

1909   Birth of Simone Weil on February 3 in Paris to Dr. Bernard and Salomea Reinherz Weil, agnostic Jews. Enjoys happy childhood in well-educated and cultivated atmosphere.

1919–1925   Studies at Lycée Fénelon and Lycée Victor Duruy. Close relationship with older brother André, a prodigy in mathematics.

1925–1928   Student at Lycée Henri IV, where she is profoundly influenced by her philosophy professor, Alain.

1928–1931   Student at Ecole Normale Supérieure, where she gains reputation as intransigent revolutionary (the "red virgin"). Writes thesis on *Science and Perception in Descartes* and is awarded the *agrégation* degree.

1931–1934   Professor of philosophy at lycées of Le Puy, Auxerre, and Roanne. Teaches in workers' free university in Saint-Etienne. Involved in controversial labor struggles, especially in Le Puy. Writes articles on labor problems, social oppression, and pacifism.

1934–1935   During leave of absence from teaching, becomes factory worker in Paris with Alsthom, Carnaud, and Renault companies in order to have the direct experience of the oppression and affliction she is writing about.

1935–1936   Teaches philosophy at Bourges, writes on industrial reforms.

1936–1937   Volunteers for noncombatant service in Spanish Civil War. Sustains severe burns. Obtains medical leave of absence from teaching.

1937–1938   Teaches philosophy at Saint-Quentin. Severe headaches, poorly healed burns, and general ill health force another leave of absence. Spiritual crisis, culminated by mystical conversion experience: "Christ himself came down, and he took possession of me."

1939–1942   Living with her parents in Paris, Vichy, and Marseilles, evolves from pacifist to resistance activist. Works in grape harvests of the Ardèche, where she meets farmer-philosopher Gustave Thibon. Also meets Father Joseph-Marie Perrin. These two friends will become literary executors and posthumously publish the first fruits of this feverishly productive period of her writing in *La Pesanteur et la grâce (Gravity and Grace)* and *Attente de Dieu (Waiting for God)*.

1942   May: leaves Marseilles with parents for New York. November: leaves New York alone for England.

1943   Works for Ministry of Interior in De Gaulle's Free French movement. Writes *L'Enracinement (The Need for Roots)*. April: hospitalized in London with tuberculosis and severe exhaustion, complicated by anorexia. August 24: death in Ashford, Kent.

Chapter One
Activist, Saint, Heretic
The Life and the Work

Simone Weil, like many other literary and philosophical figures of twentieth-century France, lived a life whose message, it will be argued, speaks even more eloquently than her writings. A writer who addresses herself to the pressing political and ideological dilemmas of her contemporary world does not write in a vacuum. Action and thought in such an individual come together in a subtle blend; neither can be granted primacy over the other. To contemporaries, the life of such a person often speaks more authoritatively than her words, while for posterity there is a unique value inherent in the writings. A life of authentic social commitment may become obscured, distorted, or even lost in the swirl of historical events that surround it. But lucid philosophical statements preserve the true character and integrity of one's actions. Biographies of Simone Weil contain almost as much philosophical discourse as historical narrative. Her biographers have found it impossible to recount her existential drama without interpreting it at length through the perspective of her writings. Conversely in this study, concerned chiefly with her written works, I find it useful to place her philosophy in the context of her historical commitments.

Born of agnostic Jewish parents, Simone Weil is claimed by some as a martyr and saint of the Christian faith. Others would prefer to label her a heretic, a Marxist revolutionary (she was known by some in her university days as "the red virgin"), or a misguided would-be prophetess. All students of her life and works, however, seem to share a common view of her moral impact. They see her life and her writings as the compelling expression of a message. People read books by or about Simone Weil, it seems, because they seek to learn a profound lesson about truth.

In researching this book, for example, I met in Paris a couple who are among the most active members of the "Association pour l'étude de la pensée de Simone Weil." I found that, as is so often

1

the case with Weil enthusiasts, they had no "professional" link to
Simone Weil studies. They were neither scholars, priests, nor activists. Their profound interest in her work stemmed rather from a
genuine, spontaneous kinship of spirit that they sensed immediately
upon discovering her writings. I was impressed with their personal
testimony that Simone Weil is a writer "who has made life a little
less difficult to live."

Paris Childhood

Jacques Cabaud and Simone Pétrement have amply documented
the brief life of Simone Weil in their biographies. The latter draws
on fuller material and would have to be called the definitive study
of Weil's life, although Pétrement's close friendship with the writer
is the source of both strengths and weaknesses in the book. In the
case of a life as saintly and heroic as Simone Weil's it is an inevitable
temptation to lose something of the objectivity that is necessary for
a balanced appreciation.

Simone Weil was born in Paris, 19 boulevard de Strasbourg, on
February 3, 1909. Her father, Dr. Bernard Weil, was of an Alsatian
Jewish family and a confirmed atheist. Mme Weil, née Salomea
Reinherz, came from a highly cultivated Jewish family who had
lived in Russia for twelve years. Mme Weil was born at Rostov-
on-Don, but she and the other Reinherz children were Belgian
citizens.

A sickly child almost from birth, Simone Weil can be said to
have enjoyed normal health for only a few years of her life. Her
interests and her philosophical tendencies are already discernible in
incidents in her youth recalled by friends and family. At the age of
three, while looking at a picture book with stories of the Greeks
and Romans she remarked, "Is it true that Romans exist? I'm so
afraid of the Romans!" About the same time, Simone was presented
a beautiful jeweled ring by a cousin who was in the habit of giving
expensive gifts. Simone replied that she did not like luxury.

The fairy tale of the Mary of gold and the Mary of tar, as it was
told her by her mother when she was four, made a lasting impression
on the child. Simone's mother's version, as we read it summarized
in Pétrement, bears certain marked contrasts with Grimm's version,
better known as "Mother Holle." In Mme Weil's story the good
stepdaughter, lost in the woods, encounters an old woman who

invites her into her house. She is told that she may enter by either the door of gold or the door of tar. The door of tar seems quite good enough to her, and as she enters she is showered with gold. When she returns home with her newfound riches, her stepmother decides to send her own wicked daughter to find the same old woman. But when this Mary is offered the choice, she enters to door of gold and is covered with tar. Simone Weil has said that in retrospect she sees the fairy tale's lesson to have been implicitly that of Christ's words: "He who would gain his life must lose it." Whereas in Grimm's version the shower of gold is a reward for hard work, in Mme Weil's story it is humility and self-denial that are recompensed.

In 1915, Mme Weil's sister Gabrielle Chaintreuil received a letter believed to be the first written by Simone Weil. Dated January 25, the letter's contents reflect the gravity of the child's preoccupations at the age of six: "Dear Aunt Gabrielle, I'm sending you this letter, for you will be very surprised; I haven't wished you a happy new year. I wish you one now. What do you think of the situation (about the war)?"[1]

Although much of Simone's time was spent reading and studying, she also showed very early in her childhood an unusual concern for the poor and oppressed. While the Weils were lodging at a pension in Plessis-Piquet, the five-year-old Simone befriended some students who were boarding in the same pension. One of the students once mentioned that because he had been born Syrian, French students did not treat him as well or like him as much as other Frenchmen. Simone was shocked and replied, "Well, so far as I can see, you are a pure-blooded Frenchman." By the time she was ten she had already been accused by a classmate of being a Communist. Her defiant reply was that she was a Bolshevik. Doubtless, Simone did not really understand the term, but at the very least it illustrated her predilection for unpopular causes, for championing those who were despised and scorned. When she was eleven, the family one day was unable to find her in the house. Their search finally ended at a meeting of striking workers, where she was helping prepare for a demonstration.

There are numerous indications during Simone's childhood of a predisposition toward stoicism that seems to have developed at a precocious rate. She always insisted on carrying a heavy load; she saved money and food to send to a soldier at the front during the war; in winter she went without kneesocks to make her legs tougher. "To a rare degree she seemed to forget all personal interest or desire and became excited only for noble causes and with no concern for herself. . . . She seemed without resentment or anger for everything that involved only herself."[2]

Family Life

The Weils were an enlightened Parisian family who spared nothing to obtain the very best education available for their children. It is clear from Mme Weil's letters (quoted in Pétrement) that they were concerned with the process of forming judgment rather than simply expanding the children's knowledge. Simone and her older brother André seem to have grown up in an atmosphere in which intellectual values counted heavily. Pétrement, who knew them well, is careful to make note of the prizes won in the lycées by André and Simone. And she says the two preferred their recitations of *Cyrano* or *Phèdre* to the games normally played by children in early adolescence.

Simone and André were very close growing up together but André was immediately deemed the more gifted intellectually. His academic record was one of brilliant and startling successes, and he was considered something of a genius, having passed the *baccalauréat* at fourteen. He was to become one of the outstanding mathematicians of his time. Intimidated by his achievements and discouraged by unsympathetic teachers in some of her classes, Simone went through a period of depression in her early teens in which she was afflicted with a deep sense of inferiority.

Two of her weakest subjects in school were drawing and handwriting. The root of the problem apparently was the smallness and clumsiness of Simone's hands. Few people, according to Pétrement, could have been endowed with hands less suited to the kind of manual labor she was eventually to undertake. Later, under the influence of her professor at the Lycée Henri IV, she came to believe that a beautiful and well-wrought handwriting would be not only a good exercise in self-discipline but an aid to sound thinking. The firm clarity of her writing as an adult is a testimony to the discipline and determination that were hallmarks of her character.

At the depths of her despair about her supposedly limited intelligence, Simone came to a new revelation. She writes that, while a student at the Lycée Fénelon, "I didn't mind having no visible successes, but what did grieve me was the idea of being excluded from that transcendent kingdom to which only the truly great have access and wherein truth abides. I preferred to die rather than live without that truth. . . . After months of inner darkness, I suddenly had the everlasting conviction that any human being whatsoever, though practically devoid of natural gifts, can penetrate to the kingdom of truth reserved for genius, if only he longs for truth and perpetually concentrates all his attention upon its attainment."[3] She comments further that although she had not read the Gospel at the time, she can see in retrospect that "the conviction that had come to me was that when one hungers for bread, one does not receive stones."[4]

All of these recollections from Simone Weil's childhood point to an exceptionally acute moral sensibility. Even her aspiration to the "transcendent kindgom of genius" was a desire to attain not only truth and beauty but goodness and virtue. Pétrement observes that already as a child Simone's deepest desires were to make something of her life and not to miss the special kind of death to which she felt called. "While still a child, she had resolutely determined to make something out of her life and she feared above all to fail or 'waste' her death."[5]

It was the good fortune of Simone Weil to be surrounded in her youth by a loving and devoted family. Friends of the Weils have remarked on the unusual warmth and closeness that characterized their relationships. However, by the time of her university studies she was beginning consciously to isolate herself from all close personal ties. "In a sense," writes Jacques Cabaud, "Simone Weil denied herself the emotional security offered her by her own family; she wanted to cut herself off completely from all that makes life easy and to dispense absolutely with comfort. She believed that this was essential to escape from the middle-class spirit she hated."[6]

Alain and Henri IV (1925–28)

When Simone Weil entered the Lycée Henri IV in 1925, she encountered the one man who was to exert the strongest and most lasting influence on her philosophy. Emile Chartier, better known by his pen name Alain, is a good example of the characteristically French phenomenon of the prominent and influential master of

philosophy. Other great teachers of philosophy in France—Camus's
mentor Jean Grenier, Proust's teacher Darlu—have enjoyed a prestige and notoriety seldom achieved by their counterparts in this
country. In the French educational system the final preparation for
the *baccalauréat* is the *année de philosophie*, an intensive year of study
in philosophy that is regarded as the capstone of the liberal education. Although Alain was actually Weil's professor a year before
her *année de philosophie*, he definitely had the greatest influence on
her thought, and she did continue to attend his lectures during her
année de philosophie. Alain's students were among the most brilliant
of his time, and many went on to prominence in the French intellectual scene at midcentury: Sartre, Merleau-Ponty, André Maurois.

While many of Alain's students idolized him to the point of
forming a kind of cult, Simone Weil's respect for him was tempered
by her basic independence. She had already begun to evolve in the
directions in which Alain's teachings then confirmed her. As is true
of many so-called philosophical "influences," it is probably more
accurately described, for the most part, as an encounter of kindred
spirits. Nevertheless, Pétrement suggests that Alain's influence may
have been decisive in certain areas of political philosophy:

> Perhaps Simone owes to him the deepening of her feeling of revolt, the
> discernment of the real causes of tyranny, and the rejection of false solutions
> that lead to an even more onerous tyranny. She certainly owed him some
> part of the lucidity and forcefulness of the thought that she later displayed
> in her political writings. Without him, she most likely would have wasted
> her devotion in the service of some political party. But in her determination
> to be always on the side of the slave she joined hands with her teacher
> rather than having formed this attitude on the basis of his doctrine.[7]

The principal points of agreement and/or influence between Weil
and Alain were their respect for the Greeks (especially Plato—
Simone had little use for Aristotle) and for Descartes, Kant, and
Hegel; an intense spirit of critical inquiry and philosophical independence; and a deep sense of the moral responsibility incumbent
upon the philosopher. They both also favored using the great literary
classics as texts for teaching philosophy.

Much has been said of the unconventional dress and unkempt
appearance of Simone, which began to develop during her studies
at Henri IV. "Her usual costume," writes Cabaud, "was a loose
tailored dress, of masculine cut, with large side-pockets that were

always full of tobacco, worn with the low-heeled shoes of a little girl."[8] People accused her of cultivating a masculine appearance, and it is true that her attire could at best be interpreted as mildly shocking by the respectable bourgeois standards of her time. Although she was very beautiful as a child, her poor health, negligent grooming habits, and increasing involvement in hard manual labor began to take their toll on her appearance in her late teens, and by her late twenties she had become a plain, bespectacled, tousled-looking intellectual. Gustave Thibon has given the following description of her appearance when he met her in 1941: "She wasn't ugly, as it has been said, but prematurely stooped and aged by asceticism and illness, and her admirable eyes alone emerged from this shipwreck of beauty."[9]

The suggestion that she made a calculated effort to appear mannish may have some substance, although it should not be interpreted as an indication of some deep subconscious drive for erotic dominance. Although her parents sometimes referred to her as Simon and she sometimes signed letters to them as "your respectful son," the masculine tendencies are probably best explained as growing out of her stoic temperament, her lack of self-regard, and her conscious acceptance of a vocation of heroic self-sacrifice. Her acquaintances became less inclined to see in her appearance a desire to be distinguished; eventually they were more of the opinion that her work left her no time to be concerned with such matters. "In any event, her way of dressing became more and more that of a poor person or a monk, who dresses as cheaply as possible and devotes the least amount of time he can to it."[10]

During the time of Weil's studies with Alain at Henri IV (1925–1928) she was already involved in social action as well as her school work. In addition to the innumerable petitions and *causes célèbres* that preoccupied the more socially conscious students, she became passionately committed to the revolutionary syndicalist, or trade unionist, movement. It was at this time that she began teaching in a kind of free university organized for railroad workers. She was to devote much time and effort to this kind of project throughout her career. It was one of her deep convictions that the proletariat should be exposed to culture and learning and that workers were capable of appreciating things normally considered the proper domain only of the privileged few.

La Normalienne (1928–31)

The prestigious Ecole Normale Supérieure has produced some of the most important thinkers of France in the twentieth century. This highly competitive school prepares its students to teach in the lycées. The Ecole Normale had only begun admitting women in 1927, but when the results of the entrance examination in 1928 were announced, there were two women at the top of the list of entering students. Simone Weil was first, and Simone de Beauvoir was second, followed by thirty male students.

In Simone de Beauvoir's memoirs, she recalls an incident that says a great deal about Simone Weil's social consciousness during her days at Normale. Beauvoir had been deeply moved by the story of Weil's having cried upon hearing the news of a recent famine in China.

I managed to get near her one day. I don't know how the conversation got started; she declared in no uncertain tones that only one thing mattered in the world today: the Revolution which would feed all the starving people on earth. I retorted, no less peremptorily, that the problem was not to make men happy, but to find the reason for their existence. She looked me up and down: "It's easy to see you've never gone hungry," she snapped.[11]

Le Puy and "l'affaire Weil" (1931–32)

Upon completion of the agrégation in 1931, Simone Weil was assigned to the position of professor of philosophy at the girls' lycée of Le Puy, a small town situated among the volcanic peaks of the Massif Central. This was the first of five teaching assignments in five different towns during the years 1931 through 1937. (The others were Auxerre, Roanne, Bourges, and Saint Quentin, respectively.) It was in Le Puy that she was to begin to acquire a reputation as a revolutionary activist. She taught at the Le Puy school for only one year, but in that short period of time the newspapers were full of scandalized reactions to her organizing activities among the unemployed working classes of the area. She was continually harassed by the municipal authorities—the mayor repeatedly demanded her dismissal—and she was arrested more than once on baseless charges. (It should be mentioned in this connection that in Weil's day and time, teachers in France were considered functionaries of the gov-

ernment. Academic freedom was not normally construed as extend-
ing to matters in which one might openly defy or criticize the
government.)

Unemployed workers in Le Puy had been reduced to working in
a municipal stone-breaking project to make ends meet during the
economic slump of 1931–32. The furor of public reaction to what
became known as "l'affaire Weil" revolved around nothing more
than Weil's attempt to persuade the city to grant a modest wage
increase to the quarry workers. When the school inspector questioned her about a police report that had been given to him, the
charges were the following: She had led the delegation of workers
to the city council meeting to present their grievances; she had then
bought drinks for them at a café; she had been seen with a copy of
the Communist newspaper *L'Humanité* on the town square; and she
had been seen shaking hands with one of the quarry workers in
public! Complaints and allegations even reached the office of the
Ministry of Education, but the rector of the Clermont-Ferrand school
district personally investigated the situation and assured the ministry
that while Simone's political activities had attracted unfavorable
attention her teaching was of a very high quality.

Weil's students at Le Puy were fond of her and loyal to the point
of circulating a petition for their parents' signatures in support of
their beleaguered teacher. Here, as in all her teaching posts, she
showed little regard for the official curriculum and refused to teach
with a view of preparing her students for the *baccalauréat,* which
she termed nothing more than a meaningless convention. Instead,
she sought to foster the growth of sound critical judgment and
required a great many short compositions on philosophical problems
that she corrected with meticulous care. It was her belief that great
insights normally come to a thinker at his writing table rather than
during moments of reflection. The results of her students in the
baccalauréat exams were predictably negative (with the exception of
the Bourges class), and she was not well liked or respected by many
of her superiors and colleagues. The students, however, were almost
maternally protective of her in general. Simone always seemed to
give more attention to the girls from the poorer families, claiming
the more affluent ones were not gifted.

At Saint-Etienne, Weil's friend Urbain Thévenon was involved
in a workers' free university project of the sort that she had helped
organize in Paris. The proximity of the town to both Le Puy and

Roanne enabled her to spend many weekends during 1931–32 and
1933–34 giving lectures to the working men of Saint-Etienne.

Auxerre and Roanne (1932–34)

Simone's trade-unionist organizing activities continued throughout her teaching career. Although none of her activities attracted
the notoriety that followed her at Le Puy, there were a few incidents
that had the effect of confirming her reputation as a revolutionary.
At Saint-Etienne in October 1933 Simone decided in the middle
of a protest demonstration at the Labor Exchange Office to address
the crowd. In a moment of impetuous abandon, she had herself
lifted to a window ledge overlooking the street, from which she
proceeded to excoriate the President of the Republic. Later that
same year she found herself leading three thousand miners in a
protest march and carrying the big red flag of the Saint-Etienne
Labor Exchange.

The life-style practiced by the young teacher during these years
was extremely frugal and austere. Her apartment was always open
to workers. She left her money in conspicuous places about the
apartment so that workers could take what they needed without the
humiliation of asking for it. She also shared her food and heating
fuel, using a bare minimum for herself. Her appetite had never been
good, and it got progressively worse with the deterioration of her
health. Her excruciating headaches, which had begun at Henri IV,
became a major problem during these years of teaching. The ailment
apparently was never properly diagnosed or treated and proved later
to make her life as a factory worker all the more intolerable. At
times the pain was so severe that she was barely able to get to the
classroom and then could manage only to listen to the students read
aloud rather than giving the lesson herself. Pétrement quotes the
following passage from a letter written by Simone to a friend in
1936:

Every time that I go through a period of headaches, I ask myself whether
the moment to die has not come. More than once when I found myself
about to decide to die, I have given up the idea from a fear of a calamity
worse than death; to a point that, to avoid the risk of succumbing under
the blows of an irrational depression, I decided never to carry through
such a resolution (save under exceptional circumstances) until after the
lapse of six months or a year.[12]

In all the towns where Weil taught philosophy she quickly sought out the peasants and workers, not only to be in their company but also to learn something about their work. She would often ask them to teach her some of their basic skills and was very proud that she could perform such procedures as soldering a joint and operating a miner's pneumatic drill. She was also able to join in the grape harvests, dig potatoes in the peasants' little plots of land, help carpenters and plumbers, and toil in the Auxerre paint works. All these contacts with the life of the proletariat, however, were doomed to superficiality, and Simone longed for a more realistic experience of the plight of factory and farm workers.

In the Factories (1934–35)

Passionately devoted to improving the life of the working class, Simone came to believe that any political theory or plan of social activism was ill conceived without a firsthand acquaintance with the moral and physical problems that confront the proletariat. For this reason she applied in 1934 for a one year unpaid leave of absence from teaching in order to pursue a project of personal study on technology and social organization in modern industrial society. For several years she had had the idea of actually working in a factory for an extended period of time and keeping a diary of her experiences. The objective was to learn by direct contact what kinds of problems most seriously undermine the quality of working-class life: physical stress, lack of technological training, quality of comradeship on the job.

The project began in December 1934, when she went to work at the Alsthom Company, a factory in Paris (rue Lecourbe) that built electrical machinery. She was able to get the job through her friend Boris Souvarine's intervention with the owner, Auguste Detoeuf. Detoeuf was an extremely enlightened businessman who eventually corresponded at some length with Weil on the subject of possible reforms in industrial planning and organization. Her work at Alsthom lasted four months; she apparently had to quit because of an injury on the job. Within a week she had been hired at the Carnaud factory in Boulogne-Billancourt, a suburb to the southwest of Paris. After less than a month she was fired at Carnaud, probably for insufficient production, and was unemployed for a month before finding work at Renault, where she stayed from early June to August 1935.

Weil's year of factory work has been called the turning point of
her life. She had always been endowed with a deep sense of compassion for the oppressed, but the experience of actually becoming
one of those with whom formerly she had only vicariously suffered
made an indelible impression on her character. Physically, Simone
was pitifully ill-equipped for the demands of factory work. Her frail,
sickly constitution, her awkward and weak hands, and her bouts
with chronic migraine headaches were enormous handicaps. She
entered the factories in total anonymity by her own choice and
refused to accept any financial support from her family, preferring
to live strictly on her earnings. Because of her constant inability to
reach minimum production levels, her pay was even more paltry
than that of her co-workers. She became familiar with the gnawing
hunger of the poor—especially when she was out of work for a
month. The humiliation of waiting in line day after day with other
unemployed workers, seemingly at the mercy of those who were
hiring, the indignities that she endured by subjecting herself to the
monotonous routine of the mechanical assembly line, the degrading
obsession with production levels and being paid by the piece: all
these hardships made Simone come to understand as she never had
before what the threat of dehumanization really meant to the factory
worker.

Weil felt that for the first time in her life she had been able to
go from abstraction to reality. It was no longer an intellectual
argument; she was dealing with real people and their real problems.
Any kindness encountered in such a world seemed a grace. "The
least act of kindness . . . calls for a victory over fatigue and the
obsession with pay. . . . And thought, too, calls for an almost
miraculous effort of rising above the conditions of one's life."[13]

Weil's most ambitious goal in her year in the factories was to
discover how one might reorganize industrial planning so as to create
working conditions in which the proletariat could become truly free.
Pragmatically speaking, the answers she found to this problem were
too vague. It was clear to her that much of the oppression of factory
workers was inherently related to the machinery they had to operate.
Obviously, a revolutionary concept in mechanical design was in
order, a design with the welfare of the worker in mind, rather than
exclusively the concern of production. But the details of such a
revolution were not clear.

The most lasting effects of the factory experience were not, however, related to specific solutions to the political and social issues that prompted Simone Weil to enter the factories. According to her autobiographical letter to Father Perrin, her experience had worked a profound and irrevocable change in her own character.

That contact with affliction had killed my youth. Until then I had not had any experience of affliction, unless we count my own, which, as it was my own, seemed to me to have little importance, and which moreover was only a partial affliction, being biological and not social. I knew quite well that there was a great deal of affliction in the world, I was obsessed with the idea, but I had not had prolonged and firsthand experience of it. As I worked in the factory . . . the affliction of others entered my flesh and my soul. . . . There I received forever the mark of a slave. . . . Since then I have always regarded myself as a slave.[14]

The social debasement of the worker's condition was the ultimate trial. The physical sufferings were real but far less devastating than the humiliation and degradation that gave her the unforgettable feeling of being a slave.

Simone Pétrement recalls that after her year in the factories she was never again an angry *enfant terrible*. "Something in her had been broken, perhaps, and her character had softened. She was no longer the 'terror,' as Cancouët had once called her."[15] Cancouët was not alone in perceiving the new tone in Simone Weil. He and the other revolutionary activists with whom she had collaborated during her prefactory teaching career—Thévenon, Louzon, Souvarine—all detected a new pessimism about the revolution in her thinking. "An obviously inexorable and invincible oppression does not bring about the immediate reaction of revolt but that of submission."[16]

Her dissociation from the revolutionary syndicalist movement occasioned by this new pessimism had actually been preparing itself for quite some time. As early as 1933, Weil had written an article for *La Révolution prolétarienne* in which she had criticized not only the Stalinist state in Russia but even the revolutionary syndicalist movement itself for excessive bureaucracy at the expense of the individual worker.

Bourges, Spain, and Saint-Quentin (1935–38)

During the academic year 1935–36, which Weil spent in Bourges, she exchanged several letters with Auguste Detoeuf, owner of the

Alsthom factory where she had worked the year before. A certain
M. Bernard, who ran a foundry near Bourges, and Detoeuf both
received detailed proposals from Simone regarding the possibility
of industrial reforms from within. One of her favorite strategies was
a proposed house organ or factory newsletter in which workers could
elaborate plans for reforms and managers could respond from their
own point of view. She submitted articles for such a publication,
some being rejected and others actually reaching the workers' hands
in print.

Weil also continued to seek farm work—without pay. One peasant woman, with whose family Simone worked for some time, has
commented on the strange experiment. Her recollections, which
must have been typical of the reactions Weil faced in the peasant
farmers she met, have the bewildered tone of a Sancho Panza trying
to take in the impossible ideals of a new Quixote. "My husband
and I used to say: the poor young girl, so much study has driven
her out of her wits; and we were sorry for her; while really it was
we who were out of our depth. But what could we do? All the
intellectuals we knew put barriers between themselves and the peasants. Simone Weil threw down these barriers and put herself at our
level."[17]

In August 1936 Simone Weil went to Barcelona to join the
anarchist movement in the Spanish Civil War. As a pacifist she
wanted no part of the killing, but the sympathy she felt for the
anarchists led her to volunteer for noncombatant service in the CNT
(Confederación Nacional del Trabajo). Although she was in Spain
only a few weeks, she witnessed enough of the conflict to learn that
neither side could be trusted very far. To her surprise, she even felt
a certain ironic sympathy for Bernanos, whose royalist leanings had
prompted him in the early stages to support Franco's effort. She
had hoped to be able to work for the cause of the starving Spanish
peasants but she soon realized that the conflict had become only the
pretext for a battle between the interests of Soviet Russia and those
of Germany and Italy.

The involvement of Simone Weil in the Spanish Civil War was
abruptly halted by an injury that would have fit once again the
image of a Quixote figure. Rather than being wounded by enemy
fire, she sustained severe burns when her characteristic clumsiness
caused her to spill boiling oil on her left leg. The wounds were ill
treated by incompetent medical personnel. Weil's general physical

condition was already poor, and the complications from her burns further weakened her so greatly that she was forced to take a medical leave of absence from teaching during the academic year 1936–37. She returned to the classroom in October 1937, at the lycée of Saint-Quentin near Paris, but by January 1938 her health was so poor that she had to apply once again for sick leave. She was never to return to teaching.

Spiritual Crisis

From the time she left the Renault factory in August 1935 to autumn 1938, Simone Weil's inner life was approaching a critical turning point. One of the first revelations of her sympathy with the Catholic faith occurred during a visit to Portugal in September 1935. A traditional procession of fishermen's wives to bless the fishing boats had touched Weil with its great, solemn sadness. Recalling the experience in *Attente de Dieu,* she says, "There the conviction was suddenly borne upon me that Christianity is pre-eminently the religion of slaves, that slaves cannot help belonging to it, and I among others."[18] During her stay in Assisi in the summer of 1937 she was filled with admiration for the pure spirit of Saint Francis. The Romanesque chapels with their Giotto frescoes and even the atmosphere evoked by the Umbrian landscapes seemed to speak lovingly to Weil's sensibility. It was in Santa Maria degli Angeli that "something stronger than I was compelled me for the first time in my life to go down on my knees."[19] Italy also reawakened Weil's poetic interests. She wrote a poem called "Prométhée" and sent it to Valéry, a poet whom she greatly admired.

Weil spent Holy Week 1938 at the Benedictine monastery of Solesmes, where she was eager to hear the Gregorian plainchant for which Solesmes is so famous. Despite the intensity of her head-aches—which made any noise painful—she attended the services over eight hours a day, meditating and feasting on the beauty of the liturgy. Again in *Attente de Dieu* she described the experience as an awareness of the image of Christ and the possibility of divine love. At Solesmes Weil also met a young Englishman who intro-duced her to the English metaphysical poets of the seventeenth century: Herbert, Donne, and Crashaw. It was George Herbert whose poems had the deepest effect on her, especially his "Love," which she often recited to herself. The poem, the Gregorian chants, and the experience at Santa Maria degli Angeli all share a significant similarity in that they began for Weil primarily as aesthetic experiences and ended up having a much more deeply spiritual impact than she had realized.

The culmination of these developments in Weil's inner life took place in autumn 1938, and Herbert's poem "Love" played an important part. "I used to think I was merely reciting it as a beautiful poem, but without my knowing it the recitation had the virtue of a prayer. It was during one of these recitations that . . . Christ himself came down, and he took possession of me."[20] Weil had always admired Christ, and from her lycée days she had read and used the Bible in her writing, teaching, and personal meditations of history, social justice, and philosophy. She had often shown an interest and even an affinity for the Catholic faith, but her hatred for Roman and Hebrew civilizations was a major obstacle that repelled her for years. From autumn 1938, however, her life was suffused with an awareness that she had encountered Christ and that she belonged to him. It was thenceforth an experiential truth conveyed to her by the person of Christ that was to guide her philosophy. In short, Simone Weil was converted to the Christian faith.

The years of Weil's spiritual crisis found her growing more and more detached from the revolutionary syndicalist movement insofar as it was regarded to be a party. Her faith in political parties had collapsed after her brief participation in the Spanish Civil War. Still, she continued to show her concern for the working class in the articles she wrote on industrial reform, and she often attended the meetings of the Nouveaux Cahiers group. Her friend Auguste Detoeuf had organized this discussion circle with several industrial executives who shared his concern for a rational and fair-minded program of social reform in factory life. An interesting footnote to literary history is that the Nouveaux Cahiers group began to meet at the Café de Flore, where the reactionary movement Action Française had met earlier and where the existentialists of a few years later were to meet as well.

Pacifism and Resistance

The new emphasis in Weil's political thought at this time was on two rather unpopular causes: anticolonialism and pacifism. The policy of gradual decolonization that she advocated was roughly the same as the one eventually adopted by the French government in the 1950s, but the French public was not yet ready to give up its territorial claims. In retrospect, the pacifist stance in which Weil persisted right up to the German invasion of Czechoslovakia in March 1939 was much less justified. She repeatedly underestimated Hitler's drive for conquest and seemed to favor the kind of appeasement policy that Neville Chamberlain was championing. Yet she was unable to approve the Munich accords, which seemed a mirror reflection of her own ideas. Almost anything, she kept insisting, is preferable to resorting to armed conflict. Finally, when news reached France of German soldiers entering Prague, Weil was no longer able to hold the pacifist line. It was much the same kind of situation in which she had found herself in 1936 regarding the Spanish crisis. "Under the stress of impending war," writes Cabaud, "Simone Weil's pacifism was mitigated by events, as it had been previously during the Spanish Civil War. In either case, she had not readily abandoned her philosophy of nonviolence. But she realized that its prescriptions were too easily reached to satisfy the demands of every situation."[21] In her *Cahiers (Notebooks)* Weil writes that maintaining a nonviolent stance depends on how far the attitude of one's adversary makes nonviolence effective. "Non-violence is good only if it is effective."[22] One must sometimes fight "because one cannot stop this war and because if it takes place he cannot but participate in it."[23]

Once Simone Weil was able to evaluate clearly the situation in 1939, there could be no doubt of the depth of her loyalty to the anti-Hitler cause. The project that may best exemplify her philosophy and the nature of her commitment to Christian and humanistic ideals is the plan that she tried so desperately to be allowed to carry out for the Allied forces. She proposed a front-line nursing squad, a group of women trained to administer the elemental, but crucial, procedures of first aid to soldiers who were wounded in battle. The group would have to be very mobile and prepared to serve a great deal of the time in the most hazardous combat areas.

The idea was practical in that many soldiers who were wounded in combat suffered severe aggravation of injuries for lack of immediate care, especially in cases of shock, exposure, and hemorrhages. The timely basic medical attention offered by such a nursing squad would no doubt have saved lives. The difficulty of implementing the plan, however, lay in convincing Allied leaders to allow women to be subjected to such extreme and constant danger as would be necessitated by the nature of their mission. She submitted it over and over again to political and military leaders, almost all of whom—including Roosevelt and De Gaulle—considered it wildly impractical, if not insane. To Weil, the project would have had at least as much inspirational as practical value. The example of the total dedication of the combat nurses would have had a significant impact in renewing the fighting men's devotion to the highest human values that they were defending. "This extraordinary project had the merit of revealing the true nature of Simone Weil's ideal-ism—a sort of moral need never to shelter herself from any struggle; a restless will to act, immediately, upon any idea that seemed to her to be good; a tendency to meet and to outdo violence and suffering by total sacrifice."[24]

Marseilles, Father Perrin, and Gustave Thibon (1940–42)

After a few months' stay in Vichy, Simone Weil moved in October 1940 to Marseilles. It was there that she first came up with the front-line nursing project, as well as another plan for active partic-ipation in the anti-Nazi cause. Hearing of the Nazis' merciless suppression of a student revolt in Prague, she conceived a plan to parachute arms and troops into Czechoslovakia. By this project, which she submitted to several political figures, she hoped to incite an uprising among the Czechs that would liberate the militant students whom the Nazis had imprisoned. She vowed that if her plan were adopted without her participation she would throw herself in front of a bus. Again her proposal was ignored. It is likely that her reputation as a Communist was an obstacle to gaining the sympathy of those who were in a position to use her plans, although she repeatedly denied ever being a member of the party.

While in Marseilles Weil attended meetings of the Jeunesse Ou-vrière Chrétienne (Young Christian Workers' Movement) and was deeply impressed with what she saw. These young workers, she wrote, exemplified a purity of spirit that was free of party mentality. Furthermore, their religion was exclusively expressed in action, and they shared her understanding of both the dignity and the oppression involved in belonging to the working class.

One of the most important associations of Weil's Marseilles years was her involvement with the group that published the *Cahiers du*

Sud, including Jean Ballard (editor-in-chief), the poet Jean Tortel, and Gide's son-in-law Jean Lambert. It was in this journal, called by Pétrement the most important literary magazine in the free zone, that Weil published her essays on the *Iliad,* literature and morality, and the special genius of the extinct culture of the Midi that grew up around Catharism. The heretical doctrine of gnosticism that characterized Catharist thought bore telling similarities to Weil's theology. The scope of Weil's syncretism in philosophy and religion was especially broad during this period, as she explored the wisdom of Indian and Taoist thought. She insisted that several major religions at different epochs shared in the supreme vision of truth: ancient Greece, Indian and Taoist philosophy, and various Christian theologies (some orthodox, others heretical).

Ever since her conversion experience, Weil had been exploring very carefully the doctrines and beliefs of the Catholic Church. She found herself drawn to Catholicism; she had a deep desire to partake of the Eucharist. But she was troubled, too, by certain Catholic beliefs with which she could not come to terms. She sought counsel from Catholic friends and from priests. During the last three years of her life she found two men whose friendship and support were invaluable to her. One a priest and one a self-educated layman, Joseph-Marie Perrin and Gustave Thibon were able to share Simone Weil's pilgrimage in a more deeply personal way than any other people she ever knew. Their reflections on this experience have been preserved in the memoir entitled *Simone Weil telle que nous l'avons connue.*

Gustave Thibon is a farmer, a philosopher, and a devout Christian. Perhaps as strong willed as Simone Weil herself, he studied Greek with her, discussed her ideas at length with her, and introduced her to the life of the Ardèche grape harvesters. In the fall of 1941 he arranged for her employment with a landowner in the region. By pushing herself to the utter limits of her physical strength, she was able to perform her work in the vineyards for the month-long duration of the harvest. Cabaud reports that she sometimes had to pick grapes while lying on the ground in order to relieve her fatigue; despite her exhaustion she still regularly worked late into the night on her writings. She tried to make the grape harvesting an occasion for deepening her meditations on the meaning of labor, and often she passed the hours of back-breaking work by repeating the Greek text of the Lord's Prayer, which she had memorized about this time.

Hélène Honnorat once asked Simone why she chose to spend her time working in the fields when she had so much within her that needed to be said. Her reply was that there were things she could not have said if she had not worked in the fields..

In 1942, during Holy Week, Weil paid a visit in Carcassonne to her university friends the Lucien Roubauds and to Joë Bousquet. She regaled herself on the Romanesque architecture along the way. The Roubauds remember Weil's appearance on this occasion to have been strikingly ascetic: clothed in rough homespun, shod in sandals, and her face wearing the absent look of one whose inner life was concerned with things beyond their ken. The brief visit with Joë Bousquet was the only face-to-face encounter of these two souls, related by a bond of suffering and a kinship of belief. Weil and Bousquet, who was confined to his bed by a war-inflicted paralysis, later followed up the meeting with correspondence that includes some of the most important letters that have been preserved in Weil's writings.

During the same trip to Carcassone, Weil also visited with two priests, Father Vidal and Father Clément Jacob, in order to determine just how compatible her unorthodox beliefs were with the teachings of the Church. Her friend Dr. Bercher had made it clear in similar discussions that he considered her ideas heretical. Although Vidal believed her to have a sincere desire for baptism he did not encourage the idea for the time being. He and Jacob urged her instead to continue to think, search, and pray about all these things. The beliefs about which she questioned these people included such things as incarnations of the Word before Christ (she cited Melchizedek, Osiris, and Krishna); doubting that the true knowledge of God is more widespread in modern Christendom than it was in certain non-Christian cultures (both ancient and modern); and doubting that God would have commanded Israel to wipe out entire peoples (as in the Old Testament account). She also had grave reservations about the doctrine of Limbo, especially because of the fate assigned to unbaptized infants.

During the final months of her wartime residence in Marseilles, Weil tried to make herself useful to the French Resistance, her most significant contribution being to help distribute the Resistance newspaper *Témoignage Chrétien*. She had come with her parents to Marseilles to await passage to the United States against her own wishes. Her preference was to remain in France and share the hardships of her countrymen. She desperately wanted to be of some practical use to the war effort, preferably under circumstances that would exact a high degree of self-sacrifice and suffering. Her gravest dread was not so much abandoning her country at a time of danger; above all she feared that she might be leaving an opportunity to serve and to suffer for others. Out of concern for her parents' welfare, however, she consented to accompany them to New York, where she hoped to be able to leave them in safety. From New York, her plan was to travel to England in order to place herself in the service of the Free French forces.

The disturbing responses of the Catholics with whom she was discussing her beliefs at this time and the months of waiting for a departure whose consequences appeared so uncertain all combined to make this Marseilles period one of especially intense introspection. Weil's meditations assumed an urgency that made her pen race to commit them to paper. Indeed, during the last two years of her life—with the exception of the few months she spent in New York— she seemed to have a growing awareness of the paucity of time remaining for her to convey the message that she felt called to express.

New York (1942)

In May 1942 the Weils finally embarked from Marseilles. After a brief stopover in Morocco their ship eventually reached New York in July. It was not long after their arrival that Simone realized how mistaken she had been to think she might more easily gain passage to England from the United States. The summer and early fall months in New York were a time of desperate discouragement for her. She began to regret the decision to leave Marseilles, especially when she learned that the political conditions there had grown tenser. It seemed to her that she had deprived herself of the opportunity to share her people's suffering.

She wrote letters to all those who might be in a position to help her get to England. It was through the efforts of her former colleague in Alain's class, Maurice Schumann, that she was eventually successful, but only after months of waiting. Her letters to Schumann give a poignant expression of her state of mind: "Pain and peril are indispensable to my mental make-up. . . . The affliction spread across the surface of the earth obsesses me and overwhelms me to the point of annulling my faculties, and I can only recover them and deliver myself from this obsession if I myself have a large share of danger and suffering."[25]

In her depression at not being able to serve the war effort, Weil wrote relatively little in the United States. She occupied herself with research at the New York Public Library on the topics of folklore and the quantum theory. She took a first-aid course in order to enhance her usefulness to the Free French forces. And she attended Mass regularly, as well as a Baptist church in Harlem, where she found what she considered "a true and moving expression of faith."

When she was finally allowed to board a Swedish ship bound for Liverpool in November 1942, she told her parents that her sadness over leaving them could not dissuade her from what she perceived as her God-given duty. "If I had several lives," she said, "I would devote one of them to you. But I have only one, and I owe it elsewhere."[26]

London (1942–43)

Since her repeated attempts to persuade Allied leaders to accept her proposal for a front-line nursing squad were still fruitless, Weil now requested that she be entrusted with a dangerous mission in occupied France. She specifically suggested such things as a sabotage job or secret messenger service. Inevitably, though, the French leaders saw her as a liability. Her very obvious Semitic appearance, her absent-mindedness, and her natural clumsiness were convincing arguments against using her, despite her dedication and courage.

Once she had arrived in England, Weil was obliged to spend three weeks at a detention camp, where immigrants were thoroughly screened for any possible enemy intelligence connections. By mid-December she was settled in a boarding house and working for the Free French movement in the Ministry of the Interior. Much to her chagrin, she was given a desk job, but she continued to beg her superiors for a dangerous mission in France. In the meantime she devoted her efforts almost entirely to the duties assigned to her by the Secretary of the Interior, André Philip. She was to submit written reports analyzing political documents received from unoccupied France. These documents, since they concerned the postwar reconstruction of the new republic, were the occasion for some of Weil's most detailed political theorizing. While their tentative nature often leads her to impracticalities and excesses, the essays in *Ecrits de Londres* offer a useful look at the practical implications of her unusual speculative philosophy.

Ever since leaving France, Weil had drastically restricted her diet in order to share the privations of her countrymen in the occupied zone. Her friends found it necessary to resort to subterfuge to keep her even minimally nourished. Her health suffered, as well, from a lack of rest. For years she had made it a practice to sleep on the floor or a table in order to limit herself to three to. five hours' sleep. She often spent the whole night working in her office at the Ministry of the Interior. These stoic habits contributed to a general decline in her health: aggravation of her chronic migraines, progressive weakening of her physical stamina, and the onset of a tubercular condition.

As she sensed the end drawing closer, Simone Weil accelerated the pace of her writing, desperately trying to communicate faithfully the message she believed to be in her charge. Throughout her life she felt obsessed by the limitations imposed on her by being subject to the temporal domain. Cabaud reports that she lived her last months in an almost perpetual state of creativity, continually scribbling down notes on random topics as they occurred to her. The *Cahiers* are full of examples of elliptical thoughts, outlines, and sketches of projects that she was unable to pursue. As such, these tentative explorations should be considered as less than central to the definitive formulation of a "Weilian" philosophy.

In April, Weil's body was no longer able to hold up under the demands she made. After having missed her at the office one of her colleagues at the Ministry found her passed out in her apartment. She was immediately admitted to Middlesex Hospital with tuberculosis and severe exhaustion. The doctors felt that her chances of recovery were good, but she persistently refused treatment and, what was worse, took food only very infrequently. She now had clearly passed the bounds of deprivation that could be reasonably attributed to solidarity with her countrymen. One can only surmise that she no longer wished to live without hope of attaining the sacrificial mission for which she had worked so long.

The letters she wrote to her parents from the hospital made no mention of her condition, and they carried the return address of her Portland Road apartment. She saw several priests, often at her own request, but she continued to mention the same reservations she had had for years about the Catholic Church. Her visitors were deeply impressed with her tranquility, her mystical detachment. She seemed already engaged on the journey away from a world where she had never really belonged.

From all the information available today, one may only conclude that despite her desire to receive the Eucharist and despite her embracing of the essential tenets of the Catholic faith, Simone Weil was never baptized. She apparently believed it was her peculiar calling to remain outside the organized Christian Church in order to continue to express her personal testimony in the absolute integrity of intellectual freedom. She once wrote to Jean Wahl that her vocation was to be a Christian outside the church.

In July, Weil wrote a letter of resignation to her immediate superior at the Ministry of the Interior, Louis Cloison. She wrote that if she were to recover and be able once again to work after the liberation she wanted to be free of any political ties whatsoever. Commenting on André Philip's remark that he could not use her intellect in his work, she wrote:

Those intellects totally, exclusively abandoned and committed to truth cannot be used by any human being whatsoever, including the one in whom they reside. It is not a possibility for me to use my own intellect: how could I put it at Philip's disposal? It is my intellect that uses me, and it in turn obeys without reservation—at least I hope this is so—that which seems to be the light of truth.[27]

Death in Ashford

On August 17 Weil was transferred to Grosvenor Sanatorium in Ashford, Kent. Eager to escape the sterile claustrophobia of an urban hospital, she was able to spend her last days in a room with a window overlooking the rolling English countryside.

On the afternoon of August 24, 1943, she fell into a coma and died at 10:30 P.M. The newspapers in the area announced that the coroner's inquest had ruled it a case of suicide by starvation, although the various medical reports were confusing and conflicting. At the age of thirty-four, Simone Weil had reached the end of one of the strangest pilgrimages in literary history. It was the answer to a prayer of self-immolation that she had prayed years before:

Father, in Christ's name, grant me this. That I may be incapable of making any of my wishes result in a single movement of my body, or even any hint of movement, like a complete paralytic. That I may be incapable of putting together by the slightest link two thoughts, even the simplest, like one of those complete idiots who not only do not know how to count or read, but have never even been able to learn to speak. That I may be incapable of feeling any kind of sorrow or joy, or any love for a single person, for a single thing, even for myself, like a perfectly senile old dotard. . . . That all this [body, senses, intelligence, sensibility, love] may be stripped from me, devoured by God, transformed into the substance of Christ, and given to be eaten by the wretches whose body and soul lack any kind of food. And that I may be a paralytic, blind, deaf, a senile idiot.[28]

Chapter Two

Ideas, God, and Reality: Speculative Foundations of Weil's Thought

Temperament

How perplexing is the blend in Simone Weil of willfulness and renunciation, of stubbornness and submission, of tenderness and inflexibility: Her personality and her thought are both full of antithesis. In *La Pesanteur et la grâce (Gravity and Grace,* 1948), her meditations on the cross, on suffering, and on obedience demonstrate how profoundly she understood and experienced the selflessness of divine love. Yet long before she had read the Gospel, the childhood aspirations to make something of her life, to accomplish something of importance for humanity, to transcend the dreaded specter of intellectual mediocrity seemed to bespeak a human motivation for self-justification. The paradox of law and grace is at the heart of both her life and her theological message. Perhaps she was given that desperate thirst for truth and justice not as an obsessive need for self-justification but as a special grace, a predisposition toward self-denial that was to be purified (albeit imperfectly) and elevated by the experience of faith and the work of the Holy Spirit.

Numerous schoolday acquaintances of Simone remember her as aloof, unsociable, lacking in human warmth. Yet the compassion she conveys in her writings and the generosity toward others that she practiced in daily life attest to an extraordinary love for her fellow man. Simone Pétrement is typical of those who read Weil's works after having known her outside the context of her writings. "Many of her old classmates, when they finally read her writings were surprised to discover that she was so human. I myself was astonished by the incredible sensitivity she revealed."[1]

Syncretism, Idealism

It is at best a risky enterprise to attempt to summarize and interpret the philosophical and religious speculations of Simone Weil. One important mitigating factor in such an effort is the unfinished, searching, *disponible* ("open") attitude that characterized her philosophy to the very end. The openness, the refusal to close an argument, defies our attempts to systematize her writings. One could make a case for throwing one's hands up in defeat and protesting that there really exists no definable Weilian doctrine. And yet, although Simone Weil was in a constant state of self-critical renewal, although the issues with which she struggled were often so ambiguous as to defy rigidly intellectual apprehension, she operated continually within the method of philosophical inquiry she had learned in school under Alain. This method, together with her passionate commitment to intellectual integrity, obliges us to call her a philosopher. An analysis of her writings must begin by an examination of the foundational aspects on which her practical philosophy rests—the speculative domain of metaphysics, epistemology, and theology.

The term most frequently used to characterize Weil's philosophy must certainly be syncretist. It enlightens us about her philosophical method, to be sure, but it obviously has no value in identifying with any specificity the particular perspective from which Weil built her worldview. A brief list of the most influential sources of ideas she used will constitute a first step toward understanding her thought: the Bible, Plato, Kant, Descartes, Spinoza, the Stoics, Taoism, Buddhism. Weil repeatedly emphasized the importance of radical intellectual freedom in her particular vocation. She felt called to serve truth above all, and the resultant *disponibilité* ("openness") entailed of necessity a syncretist philosophy.

For all the diversity embodied in the above list, we may isolate at least one methodological common denominator: an epistemological idealism. Indeed, Weil always had little use for the epistemological realism of an Aristotle, an Aquinas, or a Maritain. The logical, systematic operation of the rational intelligence among those philosophers must have appeared ponderous and earthbound to Weil's soaring mystical impulses. Like Plato, Weil's method was to begin her philosophical meditations on a purely spiritual plane, dealing with first principles, with innate ideas. Empirically apprehended data had only a secondary role. Even when she dealt with the physical world, it was either in terms of already-established philosophical ideals or as symbolic of spiritual truths.

Figurative Language, Reading, *Metaxu*

A further methodological characterization of Weil's thought brings us to a second comparison with Plato, namely, her frequent use of figurative language. Both Plato and Simone Weil were fond of proceeding toward their most difficult truths by the parabolic method. Parables, myths, and folk tales have the propensity to evoke insights in us that are ultimately ineffable. One of the reasons Weil used the Gospels so often in her writings was her great admiration for the powerful lessons contained in Christ's parables. Christ told his disciples that he had many things he could not yet tell them because they weren't prepared to understand them. He used parables because they had their point of departure in the realm of the literal, of the familiar; even though they contained priceless truths that were too rich to comprehend fully, their literal meaning was easily assimilated and thus they preserved their more secret treasures.

Weil's gift for creative intuition enabled her to seize upon Plato's myth of the cave, on Christ's parables of farm life, and on a wide variety of folk tales (Grimm, American Indian lore, Oriental folk myths, among others) as rich sources of spiritual truth. Her predilection for figurative language led Gustave Thibon to suggest that her philosophy needs to be understood as mythical rather than literal truth almost in the sense that one would interpret such mythic works as *Don Quixote* or the *Divine Comedy*. Perhaps one of the most enduring values of her work will prove to be her creative interpretations of myths, rather than the legacy of a fully articulated philosophical or theological system. One might add that Weil died so young that she hardly had the time to articulate a mature, fully integrated statement of her speculative thought.

The intuitive faculty that drew rich meanings from figurative language produced in Weil's speculative philosophy a pair of vitally important concepts that deeply influenced the orientation of her practical philosophy of science. "Reading" *(lecture)* in Weil's vocabulary refers to affective interpretation or concrete judgment of value, according to Georges Hourdin. For example, if I see a man scaling a wall in the dark, I may "read" in him (possibly without reason) a thief.[2] The other closely related concept is that of the *metaxu*, to use the Greek word Weil constantly insists on using. It refers to pure means, things that have value or meaning only in their mediating function. In Weil's idealist metaphysics, the exterior world of "things" has meaning almost exclusively as a means, a vast network of figures that can either hide or reveal the ultimate reality of spiritual truth.

The profound ambivalence of both "reading" and *metaxu* accounts in part for a certain inconsistency that is inherent in her philosophical method. Indeed, one of the most incisive maxims of *La Pesanteur et la grâce* could apply equally well to the mediating power of her philosophy itself: "This world is the closed door. It is a barrier. And at the same time it is the way through."[3] She compares man's relationship with God to that of two prisoners in adjoining cells who communicate by means of tapping on the wall that separates them. "Every separation is a link."[4] Reading deeper meanings in the everyday occurrences of life is equally risky. Forcing someone to read himself as we read him is defined by Weil as slavery. It is the existential situation of Garcin in Sartre's *Huis Clos (No Exit)* that led him to cry, "L'enfer, c'est les autres" ("Hell is the others"). The tyranny of public opinion is the root of unjust readings. She defines justice, in this light, as the attitude of being continually ready to realize that someone else is something other than what we read him to be. "Every being cries out silently to be read differently."[5]

Cartesian Doubt

A final categorization of the Weilian philosophical method is implicit in the enormous influence that Descartes exerted on her. Weil's dissertation was a detailed study of the Cartesian method, which she grew to respect greatly. Descartes's "systematic doubt" was a hallmark of her own philosophy, as well as that of her master Alain, and we see her return to it over and over in her *Cahiers* and in all of her speculative meditations. She often refers to her personal version of the Cartesian method as "le doute hypothétique," a system of testing various theories by means of hypothesizing, first their falsity, then their opposite's falsity. This tentative, trial-and-error testing of hypotheses, predicated on systematic doubt, is a variation of the scientific method and is again characteristic of the idealist epistemology. "Method of investigation: As soon as we have thought something, try to see in what way the contrary is true."[6]

The method of investigation that Weil used was an outgrowth of her obsessive commitment to intellectual probity. She was persuaded that the way to enlightenment was not to affirm anything on faith, without proof. To embrace belief in a philosophical truth that one would *like* to believe is to plunge into "the imaginary," as she called it, the realm of fond illusions. Probably because of her own tendency to desire such affirmations, she always dreaded the dangerous power of suggestion, and tried to build up a resistance to it. For example, she held that "religion, insofar as it is a source of consolation, is a hindrance to true faith: in this sense atheism is a purification."[7] Further, she even insisted that in the case of two people who have never experienced God, the one who denies God is closer to him. She had already lived out this aspect of her philosophical method as a schoolgirl. Having been reared in an agnostic family, she decided to avoid the question of God's existence, since she considered it a problem about which one could never have sufficient evidence in earthly life. It is impossible to seek God, she holds. All we can do is remain motionless and attentive, waiting for something completely unknown. At this point, before God reveals himself, we must not affirm belief in his reality. That would risk calling something else by his name and thus committing the sin of idolatry. Weil contends that this kind of refusal to believe, if the unbeliever loves God, is an equivalent to what Saint John of the Cross called the dark night of the soul. She compares it to a child who does not know there is bread somewhere but cries out anyway that he is hungry.

Guide versus Geographer

Gustave Thibon, in *Simone Weil telle que nous l'avons connue*, resists the temptation to canonize, or even to catholicize Simone Weil, noting, "We need not baptize posthumously one who was not willing to be baptized while living."[8] At the same time, he pays tribute to the aspects of her work that do deserve to be remembered. His comments on Weil's speculative philosophy are especially instructive. He finds her systematic thought weak and lackluster in comparison to her mystical insights, and he uses an extremely apt metaphor to explain the breakdown.

Between Simone Weil and a purely speculative philosopher there is the same difference as between a guide and a geographer. The geographer studies a region objectively. He describes its structures, evaluates its riches, etc. The guide, on the other hand, leads us by the shortest path to a given destination. From his point of view, anything that brings us nearer to this destination is good; anything that leads farther away from it is bad. Now, Simone Weil is before all else a guide on the path between the soul and God, and many of her statements are more profitably to be interpreted not as a description of the terrain that has been traversed but as advice to the travelers."[9]

Citing several examples of contradictory reasoning in her works, Thibon suggests that Weil's writings in speculative philosophy must not be understood as straightforward statements of ontological truth, but as a kind of "viaticum for the pilgrim of the Absolute." This way of understanding Weil's writings is already dictated by the huge influence that Plato exerted on her and the degree to which she imitated his methods in her own speculative philosophy. In an article called "God in Plato," she characterizes Plato as "an authentic mystic . . . the father of Western mysticism"[10] rather than an architect of a philosophical system. The distinction she draws between the approaches of Plato and Aristotle is a lucid one, and it is useful, in turn, as a commentary on her own *modus operandi.* "Plato's wisdom is not a philosophy, a research for God by means of human reason. That research was carried out by Aristotle. But the wisdom of Plato is nothing other than an orientation of the soul towards grace."[11]

Weil's interpretation of Plato is intriguing. It serves admirably well to undergird her metaphysical, theological, and aesthetic doctrines, although it sometimes appears a bit farfetched. She argues that the only works of Plato that have come down to us are the writings of vulgarization, intended only for the public at large. If we fail to find in these works the explicit presence of a given idea, we must not conclude that the idea did not exist among Plato and his mystical forebears. All this betrays a basic weakness in Weil's way of thinking: passionately devoted to a central vision of truth, she often was guilty of making various other philosophies fit her own, oblivious to inherent inconsistencies or adding pieces to the puzzle that did not belong.

Plato's Cave and *Attente*

Thus far, I have tried to articulate the major methodological
characterizations of Simone Weil's speculative philosophy. Turning
now to the content of her speculative thought, it is important to
keep in mind that the fundamental tenets of her metaphysical and
epistemological doctrine are often inextricably related to her theology. As Thibon implies, she is first a mystic, then a philosopher.
Her perception of truth (that which she always sought above all)
was filtered through the lens of the mystic's visionary faculty.

To the most basic of philosophical questions—What is real?—
Simone Weil replied with a long meditation on Plato's myth of the
cave. Like the cave dwellers, we are born and live in a world of lies,
shadows, appearances, and sham. "The intelligible world, or being
which is real being, is *produced by* and emanates from the supreme
Good; whereas the material world is an *artefact.*" [12] That intelligible
world cannot be apprehended by man until he experiences a kind
of conversion that Weil attributes to grace: one has the revelation
somehow that the artificial world of material things is not all there
is and that one must seek beyond it. The revelation amounts to a
conversion experience because prior to it one is in bondage to the
world of appearances represented by the shadows on the wall of
Plato's cave. One has free use of one's will only after the revelation.
From that point, the will plays a crucial part in one's enlightenment
or spiritual progress. "The prisoner freed from his chains walks
through the cave. He perceives nothing and he is in fact in semi-
darkness; and in any case it would serve no purpose if he stopped
to examine his surroundings. He has to continue walking, no matter
how painfully and although he is ignorant of where he is going. At
this stage only the will is involved." [13]

But the captive who gropes his way out of the cave has absolutely
no idea of God before issuing forth from the darkness. His quest is
a blind effort of the will seeking something of which it has no clear
knowledge; however, once he goes out into the sunlight, the will
ceases to have any important function. "No further efforts of will
are needed; one has only to remain in a state of attention and
contemplate something whose dazzle is almost unbearable." [14]

Once outside the cave, the captive, now liberated, must adopt a
new attitude. Rather than continuing to exert an effort of the will

to press forward toward enlightenment, he must now make himself open to the uplifting power of grace that comes from beyond him. Now he must passively receive, not actively seek.

Weil describes in several contexts this attitude of watchful attentiveness so richly expressed in the Greek *(hupomone)* and French *(attente)* words for "waiting." They suggest patient, expectant waiting; they connote faith, love, and stoic obedience as well. The attitude of the human soul that makes salvation possible, *attente* is defined by Weil as "the attentive and faithful immobility that continues indefinitely and cannot be shaken by any blow whatsoever."[15] The connotation of attention or attentiveness is almost as important as that of waiting, and it applies to many areas of Weil's philosophy. Her concepts of prayer, academic study, and even social justice are based on her rich interpretation of *attente*.

She is careful to point out that attention has nothing to do with muscular exertion or a concentrated effort of the will. It is, instead, a passive contemplation. Whether in prayer or in academic study, *attente* is achieved only by a negative effort: eliminating distractions and obstacles and leaving one's consciousness empty, suspended, waiting, available, penetrable by truth. *Le regard,* one's visual attention, or gaze, must be riveted unswervingly on the source of enlightenment, even as plants wait, patiently open to the all-sufficient energy communicated to them from the sun and rain. When we direct our visual attention toward an object with an attitude of openness and with no intention of approaching that object, we have achieved the virtue of attentiveness, which is a form of obedience. All this is valid, of course, only to the degree that the object of our *regard* has reality.

Various features of this new version of the cave myth and certain aspects of her thought in nearly every domain bear an unmistakable reflection of Weil's existential situation. It is quite obvious that her philosophy grew out of her life's commitments as much as it determined them. This evidence suggests that hers is a largely intuitive philosophy. The whole scenario described in the cave myth applies to the spiritual itinerary she herself followed. Two particularly good examples are what she calls *le choc du beau* ("the jolting experience of the beautiful") and the pain inevitably incurred in key stages of the progressive enlightenment.

Platonic Ascent

In Weil's life, as we have seen, there are several instances of what appeared to be almost entirely aesthetic experiences that ended up having far-reaching effects on her spiritual development. The beauty of the liturgy during Holy Week at Solesmes, the Romanesque architecture in Assisi, and especially the beautiful lines of George Herbert's poem "Love" all conform to the model of *le choc du beau* as it is described in "God in Plato," and they all lead to a new stage of the spiritual life that must bring pain. Weil holds that all human beings are born into earthly life out of a previous higher state. Their memory of the essences (e.g., beauty, justice, wisdom) that they formerly contemplated in their fullness is obscured by the corporeal nature of earthly existence. Beauty alone among those essences appears in images that may be apprehended by man. And it is only by a dispensation of divine grace that one may receive intimations of the higher order that are conveyed in those images. *Le choc du beau,* in other words, reawakens within us the memory of the divine. Hence, the Platonic tradition—coming down through the Renaissance poets, Baudelaire, and Proust—of art's inherently mnemonic nature is revived in Weil's aesthetics.

The pain caused by this experience of revelation is described in two analogies. It is like the pain of seeing something whose dazzling brightness is too much for human sight, and it is also compared to the growth pains of a baby cutting his first teeth—or of the soul growing wings. The human soul's response to the revelation of the beautiful, however, is crucial. The natural desire to consume that which is beautiful must be curbed, for "the contemplation of beauty implies detachment. A thing that we perceive as beautiful is a thing which we do not touch, which we do not want to touch, for fear of damaging it. The energy supplied by other objects of desire can only be transmuted into spiritually usable energy through an act of detachment or refusal."[16] The discipline of self-denial entails another kind of pain—this time self-inflicted—that is inevitable at the higher levels of spiritual progress. The soul now is compared to a flying chariot pulled by two horses, one representing the divine, the other, vice. The first horse overcomes the pull of gravity to climb toward heaven; the second is heavy and weighs down on the soul, dragging it toward earth unless it is properly trained. The training is painful (the discipline of physical suffering) and it entails a violent struggle *(agon)* in the soul. Here we are reminded of the painful conflict within Simone Weil as she was torn between her desire for the sacraments and her conviction that she should remain unbaptized.

The Platonic notion of a mystical ascent toward the divine is clearly central to Weil's whole philosophy, both before and after her conversion. As described in "God in Plato," it may take either of two basic forms: the way of the intellect or the way of love. It is often difficult to separate the two in Weil's writings, but in principle they do operate in two distinct modes. Again the role of intermediary is of utmost importance: "For the transition from darkness to the contemplation of the sun there is a need of intermediaries."[17] She summarizes the distinction between the two "ways" by the contrast between the intermediaries that characterize them. The way of the intellect operates by virtue of *rapport;* the way of love, by beauty.

Rapport (or *logos*) has to do with perceiving symbolic relationships, connections, analogies, bridges. It requires a creative, intuitive capability of the mind that enlightens us and helps us reach God by enabling the intellect more nearly to comprehend pure being. It triumphs over contradiction and draws the soul toward the realm of pure being. "For wherever there is the appearance of contradiction there is a correlation of contraries, that is to say, there is relation. Whenever the intelligence is brought up against a contradiction, it is obliged to conceive a relation which transforms the contradiction into a correlation, and as a result, the soul is drawn upwards."[18] The intellectual way of Platonic ascent toward God is based largely on Weil's reading of the *Republic* and is represented by the mediation of Prometheus, whom Weil presents as a Christ figure, since after stealing the heavenly fire for man he was "crucified." (She also notes Christ's statement in Luke 12:49 that he came to cast fire on the earth, along with other references to fire in Christ's ministry.) She reminds us that Prometheus is presented in Aeschylus as the author of primitive inventions, of the understanding of the seasons, of astrology and number. The connection in Greek between *arithmos* (number) and *logos* (*rapport,* "word") completes the association of Prometheus with Christ, as Weil quotes from the *Philebus:* "In Plato the One is God, and the indefinite is matter. In view of which the words: *'number constitutes the mediation between the one and the indefinite'* evoke strange echoes."[19]

The nonintellectual way, the way of love, is represented by Diony-
sos, the god of mystical madness, the god of mysteries. This "way"
is suggested to Weil in Plato's *Symposium* and the *Phaedrus*. It is a
quest for perfection. God draws the soul nearer to him in this mode
through the power of beauty. "This absolute, divine beauty by whose
contemplation one becomes God's friend is the beauty of God: it is
the attribute of God under which we see him. But it is still not
the end; it corresponds therefore to being (the Word) in the
Republic."[20]

Gravity and Grace

Very near the center of Weil's speculative thought there is a clear
polarity that consistently remains fundamental to her philosophy in
every field. It is so basic to all her ideas that she has left herself
open to frequent charges of Manichaeism. The most descriptive
expression of the polarity is the title of one of her most widely
known books: *La pesanteur et la grâce (Gravity and Grace)*. Weil draws
the analogy with characteristically figurative language. The physical
universe operates under the rule of two forces: light and gravity.
Plants offer the purest example of obedience that we may witness.
As Jesus observed, they "toil not, nor do they spin." Rather, they
remain open to the unlimited sustenance provided for them in the
light of the sun and the watering of the rain. It is not by any anxious
effort on their part that they grow upward toward the sun; this
miraculous victory over the force of gravity takes place by virtue of
a power they receive from outside themselves. "All the *natural*
movements of the soul are controlled by laws analogous to those of
physical gravity. Grace is the only exception. . . . To come down
by a movement in which gravity plays no part. . . . Gravity makes
things come down, wings make them rise: What wings raised to
the second power can make things come down without weight?
. . . To lower oneself is to rise in the domain of moral gravity.
Moral gravity makes us fall toward the heights."[21]

To fall upward toward God is the Weilian interpretation of the
Platonic ascent. Weil saw Plato essentially as a poet of grace. The
wing that powers the chariot's ascent is described in the *Phaedrus*
as a thing whose essential property is to bring upward that which
is heavy. "It would be impossible to state more clearly that the
wing is a *supernatural organ,* that it is *grace*."[22]

The sunward ascent of the soul, then, is possible only through grace, and the chlorophyll in the plant that enables it to receive the vital energy in sunlight is analogous to Christ within the human soul. Only through his enabling presence can the power of grace work efficaciously to lift the soul toward God.

Attente de Dieu—Interpretations

Attente de Dieu is one of the more accessible books by Simone Weil because it has a more personal tone than many of the others. It focuses on the pivotal moments of her life: her conversion and the resultant examination of her relation to the Church. Probably her best-known work, it is composed of letters and papers written in the first six months of 1942, just over a year before her death, and left by her to Father Perrin. It was first published by Perrin in 1950. In her theology, *attente* is the touchstone for all other concepts. It is so deeply rooted in the Christian doctrine of grace that it often anchors her extravagant flights of mystical genius.

The two titles under which *Attente de Dieu* has been published in English are suggestive of the richly varied connotations implicit in the happily worded French phrase. "Waiting for God" implies both God's absence and an expectant anticipation of his arrival.[23] It is in these terms that Weil describes her own spiritual itinerary or "wait for God" in the essay on the implicit love of God. If we start from a genuine love of truth, she states, our first spiritual discovery is that there is no absolute good in earthly existence. It is a hard lesson, and we are immediately tempted to cover it up by self-deceit. If we succeed in accepting that lesson, we turn our soul away from earthly things, but even though we are surrounded by darkness, we cannot move toward God. It is here that the patient wait must begin.

The other English title, "Waiting on God," suggests the attentive watchfulness of Simone Weil after God has revealed himself to her. She was no longer waiting for his arrival. Rather, she was trying to be faithful to him. Once the soul has had an encounter with God and has responded affirmatively, it belongs to him, and the believer's supreme desire from that point on is to be obedient to God's will. "To wait upon the Lord," as the psalmist often puts it, is to keep his way, to trust in him, to be obedient to his will. "Wait on the Lord, and keep his way, and he shall exalt thee to inherit the land"

(Ps. 37:34). Simone Weil's account of her mystical experience found
in *Attente de Dieu* is the story of an authentic encounter with Christ,
and she must be considered a believer from the point in 1938 when,
as she says, "Christ himself came down and took me." Her earnest
desire to know and obey God's will is a major theme not only in
Attente de Dieu, but throughout her writings.

One final ambiguity about the title that I will point out is that
Attente de Dieu could actually be translated "God's wait" as well as
"waiting for God." And this, too, would call to mind a characteristically Weilian motif. For her the deepest meaning of love lies in
suffering and self-denial. She carries this idea so far as to suggest
that God's act of creation was not so much an act of sovereign power
as of self-denial. For in creating a world subject to the rule of
necessity (natural law) and autonomous beings free to choose evil
as well as himself, God was limiting his own direct rule. Such a
notion of creation is not a matter of adding to what is, but diminishing it. "God and all creatures are less than God alone."[24] This
self-renunciation on God's part was already a participation in the
divine passion, a "de-creation," according to Weil. It reduced God's
role to that of a beggar humbly knocking at the door and waiting
for his children to turn their attention to him. The model of attentive, passive suffering is the immobile obedience of Christ accepting all affliction and punishment, undeserved, on the cross. But
Christ's passion began in the very creation of the world. "God denied
Himself in the act of creation just as Christ enjoined us to deny
ourselves."[25]

Malheur

One of the few most significant contributions that Simone Weil
made to Western thought was her notion of affliction *(malheur).*
And the one most important text in *Waiting for God* is probably
the essay entitled "The Love of God and Affliction." Human suffering has always been a major concern for writers and thinkers, but
few have reached the depths of insight on the subject that Weil
explored in her lifetime. She had the intellectual gifts, the philosophical training, and the genuine personal concern that enabled
her, once she came to experience poverty and oppression firsthand,
to discern the deadliest dehumanizing aspects of the working-class
life. I know of no other writer who has given us a more illuminating
picture of suffering, injustice, and affliction.

The word *malheur* in Weil's vocabulary has a particularly rich meaning. Perhaps best translated as "affliction," it goes beyond the concepts of both suffering and affliction. It is closely associated with, but not limited to, physical suffering. Only a life that has been uprooted socially, psychologically, and physically by suffering may be said to have experienced *malheur,* and the element of social debasement is the most essential. One way to convey some of the diversity of meaning in *malheur* is to list the various ways of translating its adjective form: *malheureux*—unfortunate, unhappy, wretched, poor, unlucky, despicable, worthless, miserable, pitiful, contemptible. It was this very experience that Simone Weil herself lived out as a factory worker, as a farm laborer, and as an invalid afflicted with severe physical pain. As she had learned in her own life, affliction brands the soul with the mark of slavery and cannot be understood without being experienced.

The most perilous effect of affliction is that at its most critical stages, it makes God seem absent, more remote than the dead, more absent than light in a totally dark prison; for if, thus plunged into darkness, one ceases to love God, one approaches an irremediable perdition. Throughout this, the ultimate test of the soul, one must continue to love in a void *(aimer à vide),* to love without hope of a worthy object. "If still persevering in our love, we fall to the point where the soul cannot keep back the cry, 'My God, why hast thou forsaken me?' if we remain at this point without ceasing to love, we end by touching something that is not affliction, not joy, something that is the central essence, necessary and pure, something not of the senses, common to joy and sorrow: the very love of God."[26]

And so it was in affliction that Weil discovered the love of God in its fullest meaning. Here again the ambivalence of language is a source of insight. *L'amour de Dieu* is a subject to which she returns repeatedly throughout her writings, and the expression comes to have the meaning not only of "the love of God" but also "God's love." For that is the basic thrust of all her meditations on the love of God.

Man is separated from God by an infinite gulf. Man, on his own, cannot make vertical progress toward bridging that gulf, so God comes all the way down to him. Man cannot then reascend with God, however, without sharing in Christ's suffering, his cross. He plants a seed in us that grows only through the painful eradication of obstacles to its growth within us. The seed eventually matures into a tree, the cross. There is no such thing as man's love for God; rather, the love of God for God grows within us. All we can do is diminish those things in us that impede the flow of the divine stream. "He whose soul remains ever turned toward God though the nail pierces it finds himself nailed to the very center of the universe."[27] This *axis mundi,* a center that is not in the middle but outside space and time, is the point of the intersection of the cross.

The *axis mundi* concept was one that seemed to hold a special attraction for Weil. It recurred when she encountered a similar aphorism attributed to Hermes Trismegistus (through Pascal) "God is an infinite sphere whose center is everywhere and whose circumference is nowhere."[28] And she gave it a mythic richness in the parable of the chick and the egg, one of her favorite metaphorical pictures of the ineffable experience of mystical awakening. One who has awakened to the spiritual reality of life is like a chick with gold wings that penetrates the eggshell of the world. Once outside the shell, he can love the world not from within but from the outside, from the perspective of God. "Such a love does not love beings and things in God, but from the abode of God. Being close to God it views all beings and things from there, and its gaze is merged in the gaze of God. We have to be catholic, that is to say, not bound by so much as a thread to any created thing, unless it be to creation in its entirety."[29] Love for one's neighbor, then, in the sense of Christian charity, is totally anonymous, universal, and therefore impersonal.

Anyone who has had occasion to observe people stricken with the kind of affliction Weil describes will recognize the accuracy with which she depicts one of the most detestable effects of *malheur,* namely, the vicious-cycle phenomenon, which makes it tend toward self-perpetuation. Affliction hardens one's soul and makes one feel an abysmal, desperate self-loathing, because it marks the soul with a "sense of guilt and defilement that crime logically should produce and actually does not. Evil dwells in the heart of the criminal without being felt there. It is felt in the heart of the man who is afflicted and innocent. Everything happens as though the state of soul suitable for criminals had been separated from crime and attached to those who are afflicted."[30] Weil cites Job's cries of innocence as an example of an innocent man whose affliction begins to make him feel guilty. He protests precisely because he cannot quite convince himself of his purity.

Affliction is above all anonymous and impersonal, completely random. It strikes the pure in heart as well as the faithless. It is a function of blind necessity that robs its victims of personality and makes them into things. And finally, affliction may be understood as distance from God, the crucifixion being the greatest possible distance from him.

Obstacles to Baptism

One of the most controversial issues surrounding the story of Simone Weil and her writings is her relation to the Catholic Church and the Christian faith. Thibon has cautioned against two closely related dangerous tendencies among those who approach Weil from the perspective of the Christian faith. On one hand, one may be tempted to reject her message completely because of her intransigent insistence on certain unorthodox, if not heretical, points. On the other hand, one may be so taken with her sincerity and dedication as to swallow everything she teaches indiscriminately. Marie-Magdeleine Davy accuses Perrin and Thibon of having interpreted Weil's thought from too narrowly Catholic a viewpoint, and she singles out a vocabulary problem that complicates the whole matter. She contends that Weil's frequent use of the word "God" has a wider significance than the Christian doctrine of God the Father. "For her it denotes transcendence, but a transcendence that is beyond the religions that interpret it."[31] The point is well made, for even though Weil apparently narrowed her allegiance to the Christian faith by often repeating that she loved Christ and even that she belonged to him, she believed in other incarnations of the Word, expressing herself in analogous terms regarding Christ, Buddha, and Krishna to the end of her life. (See references in letters to her parents in spring 1943 printed in *Ecrits de Londres*.)

The syncretism of Simone Weil's theology entails both strengths and weaknesses. It accounts in part for her refusal of baptism and the peculiar conception of her vocation that she maintained to the end. Like Maritain, she called for a new sainthood in our time. But the novelty of the sainthood she proposed was certainly more radical than that of the great Thomist philosopher. She compared herself to the bell that calls people to the church without ever entering. Perhaps her most intense motivation was obedience: she was unshakable in her determination to do what she believed to be God's

will for her. If we are attentive to God, she believed, he gives us
a compulsion in one direction or another, which we must follow
faithfully, neither farther nor less far than he leads.

She explained to Father Perrin that several obstacles kept her from
entering the Church: her own supposed unworthiness, her belief
that it was not God's will, and her belief that her vocation would
not allow it. Her vocation, as she saw it, was to unite herself
anonymously to various human groups in order to come to know
and love them as they are. She did not think she could bear to cut
herself off from "the huge, wretched mass of unbelievers."[32]

In order to fulfill her vocation, Simone Weil believed that she
could not enter the Church, as desperately as she desired to partake
of the sacraments. Baptism for her would have been a way of turning
her back on too many things and too many people ordinarily considered outside the visible Church. The word "catholic," she held,
meant that Christianity should include all vocations without exception, even certain heresies and "pagan" civilizations for which she
felt a special affinity. If she could remain at the threshold of the
Church, she hoped that she would be able to witness more effectively
to those outside the Church, whom she felt particularly called to
serve. The goal of this new sainthood, then, would be to manifest
to the world the possibility of a "truly incarnate Christianity." The
broad inclusiveness of her radical incarnationism—sometimes interpreted as a Spinozist tendency in her thought—indicates a readily
discernible kinship with the radical theologies of the 1960s that
grew out of Nietzsche, Kierkegaard, Tillich, and Teilhard. It is no
accident that one exponent of the "death of God" theology coined
the phrase "Christian atheism." The radical incarnationism of Thomas
Altizer's *The Gospel of Christian Atheism*[33] is closely related to Weil's
understanding of *athéisme purificateur* ("atheism as a purification")
and to the worldview expressed in the following: "There is not any
department of human life which is purely natural. The supernatural
is secretly present throughout. Under a thousand different forms,
grace and mortal sin are everywhere."[34]

The history of the Roman Church's harsh dealings with heresy
was also repulsive to Weil. The frequency with which Rome down
through the ages had pronounced the fatal words *Anathema sit*[35]
made her more than loath to adhere to that religion. One should
see in such an attitude not a fear of condemnation of her own beliefs
so much as her characteristic tendency to identify with victims of

injustice. It is related, as well, to what she called the misconception of the Church as a social entity. Indeed, Weil had a deep mistrust for any human group that tended to use the word "we" too often. She could never approve of the kind of factional loyalty she found in some Catholics that could only be compared with the party spirit in the political domain. "I am afraid of the Church patriotism existing in Catholic circles."[36] The Church, she believed, should be characterized by an openness to the world, not by social barriers or territoriality. The Christian's attitude toward the world should be patterned after the image of the crucified Christ, whose arms stretch out to embrace mankind.

At the root of all these obstacles to membership in the visible Christian Church there was Weil's desperate desire for truth, her passionate devotion to the goal of absolute intellectual integrity. Adhering to a political party, a religious community, a social class, even a family—that is to say, embracing the security of membership in any collectivity whatsoever—would have been in her eyes a grave compromise of her God-given vocation. It is for this reason that she so violently disapproved of Pascal's theology. She could not accept his belief that one should pray for faith. That Pascal's journey began as a search for God was what especially bothered her. And she rankled at Pascal's statement that "man would not be seeking God if he had not already found him." "Man has neither to seek," she insists "nor to believe in God. All he must do is to refuse his love to anything other than God."[37]

The fable that seemed to illustrate this whole line of anti-Pascalianism for Weil is the story of the brave little tailor who defeated the giant in a test of strength by throwing a bird into the sky. The giant had thrown a stone so high that it seemed it might stay in the air. But without wings it had to fall back to the ground. The dialectic of gravity and grace needs no more graphic illustration.

Implicit Love of God . . . the Eucharist

In *Attente de Dieu* there are three essays grouped under the heading "Implicit Forms of the Love of God." The first two, "Love for One's Neighbor" and "Love for the World Order," will be treated in chapter 3. The third, "Love of Religious Practices," is still another indication of the syncretist nature of Weil's theology. She recalls that the Buddha was said to have promised to bring to paradise all those who repeat his name desiring to be saved by him. Thus, for Weil, the recitation of God's name was to have the effect of transforming one's soul. All religion, she concludes, all liturgy is a form of the recitation of God's name and has saving power for all who practice it with that desire. "Each religion is an original combination of explicit and implicit truths; what is explicit in one is implicit in another."[38]

In these meditations on "implicitly" Christian religions, Weil appears too eager to find unity among essentially diverse creeds. She would have been hard put to square them with certain of Christ's unequivocal statements in the Gospels (e.g., "I am the way. . . . No man comes to the Father but by Me. . . . Not all those who cry 'Lord, Lord' will be saved"). At times her conception of the foundation of religion even takes on an excessively cultural character, which is surprising in one so devoted to truth. She suggests that if one is born into a religion that is not too unfit for the proper recitation of God's name, and if one loves that religion, one should not change religions unless obedience demands it. Her hesitancy to favor changing religions was apparently involved in her notion of rootedness. Religious conversion, for Weil, entailed a violent severing of deep cultural ties that feed one's spirit as well as one's mind.

Given the passionate devotion to the Eucharist that Simone Weil displayed in the last years of her life, it is surprising to find what an unorthodox interpretation of this doctrine she had. Father Bruckberger is representative of a number of Catholic readers who tend to assume rather uncritically that Weil uses doctrinal terms in the same sense in which they understand them. For example, unless his theology is shaky, he is mistaken in claiming that Weil "believed the same thing as I about the Eucharist."[39] Weil rejects the Roman Catholic doctrine of the real presence of the body and blood of Christ in the communion elements as absurd. She interprets the Eucharist as a convention. But one should understand that the word "convention" carried no negative connotations with her. Indeed, it refers to a miraculous power in religious life. The power of all religions, she argues, lies in the conventional purity and efficaciousness of their liturgies and disciplines.

A convention is a means of dealing with reality through signs or symbols. The convention has no particular worth in itself, but only insofar as it represents and therefore makes present in conventional form the reality it is designed to convey. Its efficaciousness, furthermore, is totally dependent upon a kind of faith in, or acceptance of, its symbolic virtue. If I pay for a purchase with paper money, it is normally regarded as a vicarious presence of the purchasing power of the gold it represents. But if the seller fails to recognize the conventional value of the paper—say, in a foreign country—the transaction is nullified. Similarly, if I am driving along the highway and encounter a road sign warning of a slippery bridge, I perceive the vicarious presence of the bridge and react accordingly. But if a driver sees the same sign without being able to interpret its meaning, it has no conventional value for him. These principles rejoin those of reading *(lecture)* and of *rapport,* as Weil understood them in their wider philosophical sense.

Transfer

One of the fundamental concepts in Weil's understanding of the conventional power of religious practices is that of "transfer." Combined with her notion of *attente,* it forms the basis for her well-articulated interpretations of prayer and of the Eucharist. Weil observes that when we are conscious of evil within us, we are revolted by it and push it out onto whatever is around us. But our surroundings, thus sullied by our evil, reflect the evil on us once again in an augmented degree. In this way we multiply evil, and we begin to feel imprisoned in evil by our surroundings. By the same token, an invalid hates his hospital room, a convict his prison cell, and even a worker his factory. This augmenting transfer principle holds true for anything that is not altogether pure.[40] On the other hand, whatever is pure absorbs and destroys evil by refusing to reflect it.

Man is able to be relieved of sin by contemplating what is perfectly pure; hence the conventional efficaciousness of the Eucharist and of the recitation of the Lord's Prayer. These are two of the religious practices Weil believed to be perfectly pure because they are a perfectly clear reflection of the person of Christ. That act of attention is what saves. It resembles the act of watching, of listening, of the bride's saying yes—attention and consent. But this quiet attention or contemplation (analogous to the passive fruition of plants) is also a violently painful act, because the mediocre part of the soul revolts against its certain destruction and invents all sorts of lies in order to avoid contact with the pure.

Simone Weil believed that one of the surest signs of purity was the willing acceptance of suffering, of affliction, of *malheur*. That explains, to a great degree, her devotion to Christ. She had the deeply intuitive understanding of grace to see that the only way to overcome evil is to absorb it within that which is pure. To pray, in the deepest sense of the word, then, is to contemplate purity, in the person of Christ, with all our attention, and to allow him to absorb the evil in us. The same is true for the Eucharist, which affords a richer, more accessible symbolism in the form of ritualistic gestures and visible symbols. Weil took all this even further, in accepting the mystics' challenge to imitate Christ. The Christian life, she believed, should involve the kind of sacrificial obedience that refrains from the temptation to reflect evil and aspires to absorb it through the willing acceptance of affliction.

Weil's meditations on the subject of eternal life and salvation are again far from orthodox, but they contain a tonic much needed in contemporary Christian theology. What should the Christian think of eternal life? Or better still, should the Christian think of eternal life at all? Not too longingly, she seems to suggest. To desire one's salvation is wrong, Weil believed. It is wrong not only because it is selfish but also because it binds the soul to a single contingent possibility. The soul is meant rather to attain a plenitude of being, which, since it is noncontingent, may not be apprehended at the same level as the human concept of salvation. In other words, the intrinsic value of salvation is diametrically opposed to eternal life as a reward for faith. Faith, thus understood, is not a voluntary, rational adherence to a body of doctrine with certain benefits promised in return. It is a gratuitous act, a blind, irresistible leap of pure freedom unsullied by ulterior motives. It is made possible by the moment of insight (a gift of grace) in which the human soul empties itself of self and receives justification.

Similarly, Weil insists that we are not called to choose good. If we attain an attitude of perfect indifference to good and evil, good will automatically win out in our souls. Therein lies the essence of grace. "A divine inspiration operates infallibly, irresistibly, if we do not turn away our attention, if we do not refuse it. There is not a choice to be made in its favor, it is enough not to refuse to recognize that it exists."[41]

The question is, if we empty ourselves of self, will the void thus created always be filled by God's justification, or is it possible to be filled with demonic power unless we go one step further (namely, to call upon God to enter)? Is faith wholly passive or do we first empty ourselves and *then* make the affirmative act, the voluntary, willful choice of God? It may be instructive to recall, in this connection, the story that Christ told (in Matthew 12) of the unclean spirit that had been driven out of a soul. When it returned and found the exorcised soul yet unoccupied, it called seven more demons to come and live there.

Last Text

In assessing Weil's relation to the Catholic Church, it is especially important to consider her *profession de foi,* or *dernier texte,* as it is sometimes called. Believed to be the last thing written by her, perhaps as late as her stay in the Grosvenor Sanatorium in Kent, it is an attempt to clarify the form into which her beliefs had evolved before her death. It begins with a clear, strong affirmation of faith in the basic tenets of the Christian religion. "I believe in God, the Trinity, the Incarnation, the Redemption, the Eucharist, and the teachings of the Gospel."[42] There, however, the affirmative tone ends. Almost all the rest of her statements express limitations of ecclesiastical authority over her individual integrity of conscience and lists of doctrines she cannot accept. One further essential point upon which she insists is that she does not affirm the above-mentioned tenets as one affirms the reality of observable facts. Rather, she adheres to them with love. "I adhere with love to the perfect, elusive truth hidden within these mysteries, and I try to open my soul to it in order to let its light penetrate within me."[43]

She further says that she has never felt herself led by God to ask for baptism and does not intend to, although her desire for the sacraments continues to grow stronger. A parenthetical conclusion expresses some apparent exasperation, if not bitterness, toward the Church for requiring acceptance of dogmatic statements from the Councils as a prerequisite for baptism. These, she argues, are not *de foi stricte.* Finally, she suggests that the Church should clearly proclaim that embracing certain mysteries with one's heart *(une adhésion de coeur)*—and those mysteries, of course, are the same ones listed in the beginning of her profession of faith—is the only prerequisite to baptism. "In that case Christian faith, without any danger of tyranny exerted by the Church over any one's mind, could

be placed at the center of secular life and each of the activities that
compose it, and could impregnate everything, absolutely everything, with its light, the only Way of salvation for the miserable
men of today."[44]

In light of all the obstacles that separated Simone Weil from the
institutional church even up to the last days of her life, it would
be an obvious error of judgment to claim her as a Catholic writer.
Many, no doubt, will even contest my conclusion that she was a
Christian. The *dernier texte* seems to suggest that her vocation not
only entailed remaining at the threshold of the Church in order to
call the "immense, suffering mass of unbelievers" to the salvation
within, it also led her to remain there in order to call those within
to a new order of saintliness and to call the institutional church to
a renewal that would favor what she called a truly incarnate
Christianity.

Weil's determination to avoid a sectarian, narrowly doctrinal
perspective made for a remarkable universality in her writings. She
appeared equally devoted to three causes: man, God, and truth. Her
vision was not always clear, but her intellectual integrity was above
reproach; it makes the celebrated sincerity of an André Gide seem
almost shallow by comparison. At bottom, it was out of humility
that she held to her beliefs so tenaciously; hence the unusual strength
and depth of her devotion to truth.

Chapter Three
The Need for Roots: Weil's Sociopolitical Thought

The opening chapter of this book was entitled: "Activist, Saint, Heretic," for Simone Weil was, in some sense and at one time or another, all of these. But the first characterization is perhaps the only one that could be applied to her entire life. Her need to share human suffering was so deep that it led her to an unusually intimate acquaintance with social oppression. She shared it, understood it, and fought it throughout her remarkable life. As her best interpreters have clearly perceived, Weil's profound understanding of the spirituality of labor and the role of suffering and affliction in society makes her sociopolitical thought a most enduring philosophical contribution. An integral part of her mission or vocation, the Weilian sociopolitical vision is most coherently and systematically articulated in *L'Enracinement* (*The Need for Roots*, 1949), on which the present chapter will draw heavily.

Toward the Ideal Society

L'Enracinement is the only book of any great scope that she conceived and wrote in one unit and during a specific, limited period of time. It is regarded by many as the most brilliant and important of her works. Written while she was with the Ministry of the Interior in De Gaulle's exiled Free French forces, *L'Enracinement* is an extended meditation on the problems of rebuilding a just society in France after the liberation. It develops in more detail than anywhere else in Weil's writings the implications of implementing her ideas on social justice, but the stamp of her intransigent idealism is ever present in these pages. No doubt, her employers at the Ministry put little stock in these odd and impractical schemes, bent as she was on an uncompromising pursuit of truth and justice. It has been suggested that they may have assigned her the project primarily in order to keep her busy and divert her attention from the *idée fixe* of being given a dangerous mission in occupied France. To be sure, her refusal to accept the demands of expediency gives her political theories a utopian quality that would have been foreign to those aspiring to political power.

Yet her fierce idealism was tempered by a healthy pragmatism. Her insistence on living out the implications of her thought and her concern for its effectual implementation made for a sociopolitical philosophy that began in the rarefied atmosphere of Platonic myths and metaphysical insights but was always followed up by a realistic plan of action. In her "Reflections Concerning the Causes of Liberty and Social Oppression," she gives a clear picture of the relation between real action and the ideal:

The time has come to give up dreaming of liberty, and to make up one's mind to conceive it. Perfect liberty is what we must try to represent clearly to ourselves, not in the hope of attaining it, but in the hope of attaining a less imperfect liberty than is our present condition; for the better can be conceived only by reference to the perfect. One can only steer towards an ideal. The ideal is just as unattainable as the dream, but differs from the dream in that it concerns reality; it enables one, as a mathematical limit, to grade situations, whether real or realizable, in an order of value from least to greatest.[1]

The vision of Simone Weil addressed itself to rootlessness, to dehumanization and alienation among urban industrial workers as well as the peasants in the rural farms. It proposed solutions— solutions having to do essentially with a society based on the spiritual dignity of work. To her it seemed that such an ideal was the only kind of common cause under which the civilized world could unite at the end of the war. Christians and Communists, radicals and conservatives alike would happily embrace the goal. The sufferings of her countrymen in occupied France were a source of deep pain for her; and yet, the growing prospect of the liberation gave her new hope that her vision of justice might soon be realized, at least in some measure. France was soon to be given a chance to begin afresh her long quest for liberty, equality, and fraternity. Weil's projects for the reorganization of France might serve as a model for other civilized cultures.

Declaration of Human Obligations

It is an indication of the pure philosophical ideals on which her meditations remain faithfully focused that *L'Enracinement* begins with a discussion of basic human obligations rather than rights. The democratic ideal we have inherited from the Enlightenment—and in which both the American and French republics were born—begins with the concept of natural human rights. Such a concept presupposes a kind of adversary relationship among men that must be controlled by mutual recognition of certain limits to individual freedom. Weil's dissatisfaction with the concept of rights, as opposed to obligations, is largely a matter of point of view. A political order built on basic human rights by nature encourages a selfish preoccupation with protecting one's own rights and leaving it to others to ensure theirs. "An obligation which goes unrecognized by anybody loses none of the full force of its existence. A right which goes unrecognized by anybody is not worth very much."[2] Each individual, then, must begin the quest for a just society not by demanding his rights but by recognizing his obligations toward others. It is the same principle—though on a higher philosophical plane—in which John F. Kennedy's famous words were grounded: "Ask not what your country can do for you; ask what you can do for your country."

Simone Weil's utopia is an ideal built on the visionary power of selfless love, the same noble, giving spirit she saw in Plato, Christ, and the Stoics. Despite the fact that she uses the word "respect," her description of it would appear to call for the notion of love. "The fact that a human being possesses an eternal destiny imposes only one obligation: respect. The obligation is only performed if the respect is effectively expressed in a real, not a fictitious, way; and this can only be done through the medium of Man's earthly needs."[3]

Love, in the sense of charity, is freely given and extends, if it is pure, to all men in like manner, regardless of merit. Respect, on the other hand, is earned. One has little respect for a poor man who makes no effort to provide for his family, but one's love for him as a fellow human being is expressed in the attempt to help him feed his family.

Need for Truth

Aleksandr I. Solzhenitsyn in *The Oak and the Calf* speaks with bitter indignation of Russian writers who have compromised with the Soviet government's policy of intellectual tyranny. He asserts that in spite of their natural talents they will never reach their artistic potential, for their compromise amounts to a tacit conspiracy never to speak the truth. Truth was never an abstraction for Simone Weil; she even insisted that it was not an object to be loved. Reality is the object to be loved. Truth is the relation of reality to the attentive, honest mind. As with her friend Gustave Thibon, truth was something above all to be lived: "To desire truth is to desire direct contact with a piece of reality."[4] "This direct contact," says Alfred Kazin in a fine essay on *L'Enracinement*, "was the one aim of her life, and her ability to find it in the darkest, most unexpected places is her special gift to a generation for whom, more than for any other, the living world has become a machine unresponsive to the human heart."[5]

Truth, according to Weil, is the deepest and most sacred earthly need of the human soul. For that reason she advocates the creation of special courts that would have the authority not only to condemn "avoidable errors" in the press but to impose prison sentences on repeated offenders. Ignorance, she warns, is not a valid excuse. "A switchman responsible for a train accident and pleading good faith would hardly be given a sympathetic hearing."[6] How much more should journalists be held responsible for the degree to which they misinform or prejudice the public! Propaganda and tendentious reporting, she suggests, must be rigorously banned from news broadcasts and the daily press. Editorializing or persuasive journalism should be relegated to journals that appear no more often than weekly.

The need for truth is the most important of the "needs of the soul" in Weil's philosophy because it is intimately related to the concept that forms the essential basis of her social and political thought, the notion of rootedness *(l'enracinement)*. To feel that one is at home, to feel that one belongs, that one has inherited one's own distinctive traditions, memories, and beliefs can be of crucial importance in the search for identity. We are what we are, thanks to the cultural, religious, and social character of our ancestors, as well as the influences of our present milieu. Rootedness is defined by Weil as "real, active, and natural participation in the life of a community which preserves in living shape certain particular treasures of the past and certain particular expectations for the future."[7] There seems to be a close relationship among rootedness, culture, and education. Rootedness is the preserving of values, ideas, treasures of the mind and of the spirit. It is repeatedly described in her writings in terms of a kind of food for the soul, a source of nourishment without which one quickly becomes less than human. Once cut off from this cultural heritage, one is traumatized by feelings of loneliness, meaninglessness, and anxiety. The example of the American Negro is perhaps the most immediate in our society, but the malady of uprootedness extends in lesser degree to the entirety of our modern world. Were she alive today, Simone Weil might well attribute the whole modern emphasis in art and literature on meaninglessness and alienation to the frustrated need for roots.

Uprooting Forces

The means of preserving and expressing one's cultural heritage is the social group *(collectivité)* to which one belongs, whether it be one's country, one's family, or one's religious community. The things that sever people from the source of their cultural heritage in the most violent and obvious ways include military conquest, genocide, slavery, political oppression, religious persecution, and deportation. However, there are much more insidious and sometimes equally devastating forces at work to uproot whole peoples.

When a culture's system of social, industrial, or legal organization is so poorly planned as to multiply the incompatibility of various imperative duties, one "is made to suffer in his love of good."[8] Hence, a basic need of the human soul is that of order. So one of the prominent uprooting factors in the modern world is the abundance of political entities in which order is not served by the sociopolitical system. The tyranny of money in modern industrial society is even more dangerous than disorder or military conquest. "Money destroys human roots wherever it is able to penetrate, by turning desire for gain into the sole motive. It easily manages to outweigh all other motives, because the effort it demands of the mind is so very much less. Nothing is so clear and so simple as a row of figures."[9] The most tragic example of the phenomenon for Weil is the assembly-line worker who is paid "by the piece," or proportionate to the quantity of a given item produced by repeating the same mindless procedure *ad nauseam*.

Education, whose task is properly to cultivate the rootedness of a society, has shown since the Renaissance an alarming tendency to perform the very opposite function. The cultural content that it seeks to convey has been reduced to a confined atmosphere, divorced from the real world, and dominated by the demands of technology,

pragmatism, and specialization. "What is called today educating
the masses is taking this modern culture, evolved in such a closed,
unwholesome atmosphere, and one so indifferent to truth, removing
whatever it may still contain of merit—an operation known as
popularization—and shoveling the residue as it stands into the
minds of the unfortunate individuals desirous of learning, in the
same way as you feed birds."[10]

Oppression and Liberty

Oppression in all its forms has to do with the arrogation of
privilege by the powerful to the exclusion of the weak. The power
through which oppression is inflicted is a form of the invisible evil
that Weil calls gravity. She is in agreement with Marx on his analysis
of oppression in industrialized society and his indictment of the
capitalist system. Her own solutions to the problem of oppression,
however, bear little resemblance to Communist doctrine, and she
accuses Marx of a kind of naive messianism in his plan for a revolutionary progress toward the full enfranchisement of the proletariat.
"The word 'revolution' is a word for which you kill, for which you
die, for which you send the labouring masses to their death, but
which does not possess any content."[11]

The most profound fallacy of Marxist doctrine, according to Weil,
is the absurd hope that a materialistic world, under the absolute
sway of gravity, can one day be transformed into a vision of justice
without the agency of divine grace. "Marx's revolutionary materi-
alism consists in positing, on the one hand, that everything is
exclusively regulated by force, and on the other that a day will
suddenly come when force will be on the side of the weak. . . .
The idea that weakness as such, while remaining weak, can constitute a force, is not a new one. It is the Christian idea itself, and
the Cross is the illustration of it. But it has to do with a force of
quite a different kind from that wielded by the strong; it is a force
that is not of this world, that is supernatural."[12] It is clear that the
only lasting solution to oppression, for Weil, is of a supernatural
order. The utter debasement of the cross in the eyes of the world
is the mysterious symbol of true strength, the most powerful force
in the universe: the sacrificial, selfless love that created all things.
Real progress in combating oppression, then, can only be accomplished by individuals who succeed in yielding to that power. Grace
is the only force capable of overcoming gravity.

All political power, according to Weil, is unstable; it may even be accurately called illusory, "for, through a vicious circle, the master produces fear in the slave by the very fact that he is afraid of him, and vice versa."[13] The vicious circle is repeated on an even grander scale when one considers the dynamics of domestic and foreign affairs, as they relate to preserving political power. "A power must always tend towards strengthening itself at home by means of successes gained abroad. . . . The struggle against its rivals rallies behind it its own slaves, who are under the illusion they have a personal interest in the result of the battle. But, in order to obtain from the slaves the obedience and sacrifices indispensable to victory, that power has to make itself more oppressive; to be in a position to exercise this oppression, it is still more imperatively compelled to turn outwards; and so on."[14]

The intricate relationship of cause and effect that binds the capitalist economy to an overly powerful centralized state begins in the increasingly bureaucratic nature of economic activity. Economic competition in a capitalistic system evolves relentlessly toward a kind of warfare. "The means employed in the economic struggle— publicity, lavish display of wealth, corruption, enormous capital investments based almost entirely on credit, marketing of useless products by almost violent methods, speculations with the object of ruining rival concerns—all these tend to undermine the foundations of our economic life far more than to broaden them."[15] The capitalist economy and the bureaucratic state thus fuel each other's hunger for power, and the mainspring upon which the whole chaotic system operates is preparation for war, or what is today referred to more often as the military-industrial complex.

The maddening round of oppression, which afflicts the master as well as the slave, could be avoided, Weil hoped, in the reconstruction of the French Republic. The singular fairness with which she drew up her charter for a free society in *L'Enracinement* is evident in her pairing of apparent opposites, according to the needs of the soul: equality and hierarchy, security and risk, honor and punishment, and—perhaps the most fundamental—freedom and obedience. True obedience is predicated on free consent, rather than fear of punishment or hope of reward. It is all bound up, for Weil, with the nature of man's freedom before God. The Lord created man in a state of radical freedom; otherwise, man's obedience could not have stemmed from free consent. Remembering that creation was an abdication of divine power, rather than an extension of it, one sees the sacred character of obedience in Weil's description of "de-creation" (the principle upon which she bases obedience). De-creation is defined in *La Pesanteur et la grâce* as causing to pass from the created realm into the uncreated, whereas destruction is causing to pass from the created realm into nothingness. "Creation is an act of love and it is perpetual. At each moment our existence is God's love for us. But God can only love himself. His love for us is love for himself through us. Thus, he who gives us our being loves in us the acceptance of not being. Our existence is made up only of his waiting for our acceptance not to exist. He is perpetually begging from us that existence which he gives. He gives it to us in order to beg it from us."[16]

The freedom of the individual to obey earthly authority, then, grows directly out of his freedom of self-renunciation, or de-creation, the only act whereby he may make himself more like his creator, and any affliction that inhibits man's freedom deals a devastating blow to his rootedness. "Nothing is worse than extreme affliction which destroys the 'I' from the outside, because after that we can no longer destroy it ourselves."[17] For these reasons, Weil sees grave danger in a system of authority predicated on either the fear of punishment or the hope of reward. "Those who keep masses of men in subjection by exercising force and cruelty deprive them at once of two vital foods, liberty and obedience; for it is no longer within the power of such masses to accord their inner consent to the authority to which they are subjected. Those who encourage a state of things in which the hope of gain is the principal motive take away from men their obedience, for consent, which is its essence, is not something which can be sold."[18]

Weil's special distaste for the crime of rape and for prostitution may be understood as other manifestations of her attitude toward freedom and obedience. The individual's free consent in all matters is deeply sacred for her. Oppression and tyranny constitute a rape of one's freedom, just as prostitution amounts to a debasing way of bartering off that which by its very essence cannot be sold. "The condition of [the] professional prostitute constitutes the extreme degree of uprootedness, and, in connection with this particular malady, a mere handful of prostitutes is sufficient to spread a tremendous amount of infection."[19]

All political authority is corrupted by the influence of gravity, but the degree to which it escapes the force of gravity makes it worthy of respect and obedience. The legitimacy of political power, political leaders, and political systems in general depends on the degree to which people in power recognize their moral obligations toward others and practice the filling of human needs that correspond to such obligations. Whoever has turned his love and attention toward the reality that transcends the world understands the obligation to respond to bodily and spiritual needs of all men. The profession of such obligation is usually tainted with some degree of falsehood or pretense. But even when the profession of it is sincere and true, its practice is imperfect.

The basic factor that is common to rootlessness both in the urban factories and on the rural farms, according to Weil, is the utter lack of finality in work. Or, in a slightly different sense, the world of work is regulated entirely by necessity rather than a good to be achieved. As she explains it in *La Condition ouvrière,* the farm worker and the factory worker both labor out of the necessity to earn a living rather than with the purpose of acquiring any good. It is the same kind of economic slavery endured for years by the poor share-cropper who labored all year only to find at harvest time that if he were lucky he might earn enough (after the owner's portion was taken) to pay off the debts that he had accumulated over the past year. The depressing prospect of always ending up in about the same place in still another vicious circle reduces life to a struggle for survival. The most common easy escapes from this prison are debauchery, drugs, violence, and the illusory hope of revolutionary deliverance.

Christian/Stoic Ethic

For Weil the key to virtue, to ethical behavior, and therefore, to her entire sociopolitical philosophy lay in man's capacity to imitate God's self-renunciation as it expressed itself not only on the cross, but even in creation. This voluntary de-creation, as it was termed above, is further elaborated in a passage of her essay on "Love of the World-Order." "To empty ourselves of our false divinity, to deny ourselves, to give up being the center of the world in imagination, to discern that all points in the world are equally centers and that the true center is outside the world, this is to consent to the rule of mechanical necessity in matter and of free choice at the center of each soul. Such consent is love."[20] The radical generosity of de-creation was applied again by Weil in her meditation on friendship. Her personal vocation had ruled out the possibility of romantic love or marriage, but to a select few acquaintances she was known, despite her stubbornness and eccentricities, as an unusually good friend. Her particular genius for friendship was a gift that became a source of deep insight for her philosophical quest.

She found the definition of friendship in the Pythagorians' formula: "Friendship is an equality made of harmony." "There is harmony because there is a supernatural union between two opposites, that is to say, necessity and liberty, the two opposites God combined when he created the world and men. There is equality because each wishes to preserve the faculty of free consent both in himself and in the other. . . . There is no friendship where there is inequality."[21] Thus, reciprocity is a *sine qua non* of friendship, because of respect for the autonomy of the other. Necessity corrupts and degrades friendship because it does violence to the autonomy of the other. Friendship is also corrupted to the extent that there is a desire to please, or the opposite. The friends must not desire to be united as one; rather they must accept the condition of separation. "Friendship is a miracle by which a person consents to view from a certain distance, and without coming any nearer, the very being who is necessary to him as food."[22] The consent to conserving autonomy both in one's self and the beloved carries implicit with it the desire to extend it universally, "for we cease to arrange the order of the world in a circle whose center is here below. We transport the center of the circle beyond the heavens."[23] There is even a divine indifference, an impartiality, an impersonal perfection in friendship extended universally, that echoes God's perfect justice in sending the rain on both the just and the unjust.

Weil's ethical thought remains in all respects close to the Stoic philosophy that nourished her throughout her life. Those who come to Gustave Thibon's farm in the Ardèche, where Weil worked in the grape harvest and pursued her mystic quest, are shown, among the sights and sounds that were a part of her life there in 1941, her personal copy of the Greek text of Marcus Aurelius, dog-eared from much use and filled with comments and retranslations noted in the margin. The goal of life for the Stoics was "to live consistently with nature."[24] Nature here implied both human nature, for the individual, and universal natural law, for the cosmos. The Stoics agreed that whenever the natural order of things overrides the narrower good of the individual, man must accept, indeed embrace, such apparent misfortune. The wise man's happiness does not depend on whether good or evil befalls him individually but on his own attitude toward the vicissitudes of fortune. Happiness lies in virtue, and virtue is almost synonymous with wisdom, the knowledge that the world operates in accordance with a natural order conceived by God.

To accept, and even to love, the world order (the Stoics' *amor fati*) is to be obedient to the divinely ordained rule of necessity (or gravity) in the inanimate world, according to Weil. Love of the world order, as she calls it in *Attente de Dieu,* is acceptance of God's absence in earthly life. He allows the sun to shine on the just and the unjust alike because he refuses to intervene in the natural order and allows necessity instead to run its blind course. The inanimate things of nature are models of obedience for man. Their docility to the reign of necessity is what Weil calls the beauty of the world order. "One is right to love the beauty of the world, since it is the mark of an exchange of love between the creator and creation. Beauty is to things what holiness is to the soul."[25]

Weil's "Christian Stoicism," as it might be called, is not a matter of loving the evil that befalls us; nor is it loving the good that comes our way. It consists more properly in loving God in and through both the good and the evil. Weil's illustration of this principle is the story of a child who carelessly breaks his mother's china vase. With the passing of time, if, after the child has left home, the mother happens on the broken vase, it is no longer a source of anger or sorrow, but of fond remembrance, since it reminds her of the absent child's existence. "It is in this manner that in and through all things—good and evil alike—we must love God. So long as we love only in and through good, it is not God we love, but something earthly that we call by the same name. . . . Behind every reality there is God."[26] The final sentence, which sums up with such luminosity the essence of Weil's Christian Stoic ethical philosophy, is close in kinship to the mystical insight of the protagonist in *Le Journal d'un curé de campagne* (*The Diary of a Country Priest,* 1936), whose dying words conclude Bernanos's novel: "Everything is grace" ("Tout est grâce").

In matters of choice, on the other hand, we are to act not in obedience to gravity but to spiritual necessity. Being obedient to God usually means going counter to the natural desires of man that constitute his own inner gravity. "Obedience is the supreme virtue."[27] But the choice of right action, of acting in accordance with God's will, may be reduced in its purest form to "doing only those righteous actions which we cannot stop ourselves from doing, which we are unable not to do."[28] Moral action results from truly praying, "Thy will be done," that is, emptying one's self of individual desires and passions and praying to be impelled, but without knowing in what direction. This kind of prayer enables one to attain to the pure, impersonal justice that moved the elect in Matthew 25 to minister to the "least of these," the anonymous victims of affliction, whom they did not recognize as the Christ: "Lord, when did we see you hungry and feed you, or thirsty, and give you drink?" they asked. It is what Simone Weil called "detachment from the fruits of action . . . to act not *for* an object but *from* necessity. I cannot do otherwise. It is not an action but a sort of passivity. Inactive action."[29]

Two of Weil's favorite stories illustrate the moral quality of passivity, or inactive action. They show that for her the most virtuous deeds are a kind of nonaction. The first, Grimm's "Tale of the Six Swans," concerns six brothers who have been metamorphosed into swans by a witch. Simone Pétrement's summary follows:

To restore them to human form their sister must spin and sew six nightshirts for them out of white anemones and cannot speak at all while the work is going on. She takes six years to make the shirts. Her silence puts her in great danger, for she is exposed to accusations to which she cannot reply. Finally, when she is on the point of being sent to the gallows, the swans appear, she throws the shirts made of anemones on them, and once again they assume human form; so she is saved, for now she can justify herself.[30]

This fairy tale was the focus of one of the first papers Weil wrote as an assignment for Alain in 1925. Her commentary emphasizes the purity of the white anemones, the passivity of the sister's silence, and the effectiveness of her sacrifice, and she concludes that strength and virtue reside only in refusing to act.

The second model of nonaction or abstention is the story of Alexander the Great, leading his men across a desert. When one of his men brought him the only remaining drink of water, he is said to have poured it out on the sand, rather than drink it in front of his thirsty men. "Sacrifice is the acceptance of pain, the refusal to obey the animal in oneself, and the will to redeem suffering men through voluntary suffering. Every saint has poured out the water; every saint has rejected all well-being that would separate him from the suffering of men."[31]

Against Personalism

To return to the notion of pure justice illustrated in Matthew 25 and in the two examples of inactive action given above, it is important to note that Weil emphasizes the impersonal, anonymous aspect of such action (or nonaction). The recurring model is God's pure impartiality in causing the rain to fall on the just as well as the unjust. The "personalist" philosophy so popular at the time among French Catholic thinkers such as Maritain and Mounier was perceived by Weil as a gravely misguided philosophy.[32] What is sacred in man, she believed, is not his person but what is indeed most impersonal. It has to do with the artistic and scientific faculties and with the undying expectation deep within the human heart that, despite the contrary lessons of bitter experience, one is going to be treated with goodness and not evil. More specifically, Weil seems to be talking about the unquenchable thirst for truth in man.

What Weil rejects in the personalist philosophy is its tendency toward what has come to be called self-actualization. In its most extreme form it is the Faustian impulse expressed in Blake's horrifying line from *The Marriage of Heaven and Hell* ("Sooner murder an infant in its cradle than nurse unacted desires") and in Gide's notion of the gratuitous act *(l'acte gratuit)*. It would be a travesty to think of the *Iliad*, Gregorian chant, romanesque architecture, or the invention of geometry as the fruits of self-actualization. There have been accomplishments in science, art, literature, and philosophy that were essentially motivated by self-actualization, and they are dazzling successes that place their discoverers' names in all the history books. But the things of the very highest order are in a totally separate realm, for they are anonymous and impersonal. "What is sacred in science is truth; what is sacred in art is beauty. Truth and beauty are impersonal. . . . If a child is doing a sum and does it wrong, the mistake bears the stamp of his personality.

If he does the sum exactly right, his personality does not enter into it at all. Perfection is impersonal. Our personality is the part of us which belongs to error and sin. The whole effort of the mystic has always been to become such that there is no part left in his soul to say 'I.' "[33] This emphasis on anonymity accounts in large part for a recent statement by the French novelist Vladimir Volkoff, who has been attracted to Weil's work for years because "there is nothing 'sweet' in Weil's talk about God." There is no sugar coating intended to make her spiritual insights more palatable to a decadent, hedonistic society.

Urban Rootlessness

The most urgent needs pressed by Weil in regard to the plight of the industrial proletariat were not wages. In fact, the major reform that she conceived in the course of her own firsthand factory experience was to make a radical transformation of the system of incentives for productivity. Rather than confining incentives to fear (of being laid off or moved to a more distasteful job) and acquisitiveness (and the limit of expectations here was rather low), Weil suggests that better conditions in which factory work is carried out could result in a far happier and more productive work force.

The first working condition that needed drastic reform was the design of factory machinery. Basically, the machine must be designed to serve man and not the contrary. The designers apparently had concerned themselves exclusively with the machine's productive efficiency, and the whole factory environment, as well, was built with the interests of production (and consumption) foremost in mind. No one seemed to think of the workers who would sacrifice their attention, energy, and often their very health to the operation of the machines. During her work experience, Weil was scandalized by the devastating effects of having to work with certain pieces of equipment (jackhammers that left the operator in a state of numb detachment, ovens that burned one's skin, assembly-line contraptions that mutilated hair and limbs). She suggests in *L'Enracinement* that the engineering students who will one day design factory machinery should be given a curriculum that entails a serious study of the needs of the workers who will be operating the equipment. The means of production could thus be operated in a humane fashion. To Weil, Chaplin's *Modern Times* was not only a clever comic farce of assembly-line drudgery; it was all too real in its nightmarish depiction of dehumanization in modern industrial society. One of the most important reforms in factory life that Weil proposes—and, by the same token, one of the most problematical— is the education of workers. We know that she herself was engaged in workers' universities in several towns and that she took any opportunity available to encourage working-class people to extend their learning as far as possible. Humanized factory work, she insists, is impossible without the freedom and joy that come from acquiring the riches of intellectual and artistic culture. The problems in such a scheme are mammoth: translation and transposition, lack of time and energy among the workers themselves, disharmony between menial labor and "liberal" studies. Since "liberal" studies educate men for freedom, the more they learn of such things, the harder it will be for them to accept the yoke of meaningless menial labor without hope of imminent reforms in factory life. Workers must be taught in terms they can understand by someone who understands them. Yet Weil insists it is a mistake to bring culture "down" to the workers' level because their level is actually higher than that of the educated. Classical literature and philosophy must be translated into their language, not vulgarized. Indeed, such transposition, she suggests, is a criterion for true literary genius, and the translation would be salutary for our overspecialized culture. After her year of factory work, Weil claimed that factory workers were in a better position to understand the heroes of Greek tragedy than the more privileged modern classes, and she wrote translations or summaries of several Greek texts for workers *(Antigone, Electra, Philoctetes)*.

Another rather notable feature of Weil's program is the idea of mobility. She favors reviving a form of the old *Tour de France,* a provision of the old guild system that required an apprentice to travel frequently among major centers of production while learning his trade. Abolishing large factories, Weil would reorganize production into a network of small workshops scattered across the country whose products would be funneled to a central assembly shop. Workers would all have periodic short-term assignments at the assembly shop, so that they could witness the coming together of the various components into a functioning whole. The actual work period at the assembly shop would be no more than half a day in order to allow time for technical demonstrations of how the products serve people's needs, geography lessons to explain where they are sent, and fraternizing with fellow workers. The deadly monotony of the assembly-line routine, according to Weil, makes it especially important for factory workers to be educated on the way their particular, isolated functions fit into the larger plan of the factory. If they understand the usefulness of the parts they produce, where the finished product eventually goes, and what purpose it serves for the people who will buy it, they can feel more at home in their jobs and perform them with more pride.

Weil favors the principle of proprietorship in a rather unusual way. Upon marriage and after passing a stringent examination of his technical skills, intelligence, and general culture, the worker would be awarded as a gift from the state nontransferable (or non-hereditary) ownership of the equipment he operates, a house, and the land upon which it rests.

Finally, an absolute requirement for economic justice would be completely equal freedom of mobility, both upward and downward. "To the extent to which it is really possible for the son of a farm laborer to become one day a [cabinet] minister, to the same extent should it really be possible for the son of a minister to become one day a farm laborer."[34] However, the complications of a situation such as the one described in the above passage are clear enough to Weil that she stops short of advocating such drastic downward mobility. She suggests, instead, a criminal-justice system in which punishment for crimes would be more severe in proportion to economic or political rank. This belief that privilege, rank, and power should entail grave personal risk is reflected in her proposal that postwar France be governed by a president who would be liable for capital punishment in case of wrongdoings perpetrated during his term of office. One could perhaps conclude that in Weil's utopia a Richard Nixon might have been in grave danger of being executed.

Criminal Justice

Criminal justice is one of the subjects on which Weil's insights are most remarkable. At times her emphasis on the use of punishment to "educate" in the moral sense is disturbingly reminiscent of Robespierre's self-righteous propaganda. Yet it is also obviously grounded in biblical principles of effectual propitiation, community, and equality. Paired with honor as one of the complementary needs of the soul in *L'Enracinement*, punishment is defined by Weil as the means of reintegrating into the human community those who by committing crimes place themselves outside the network of eternal obligations that bind men together. The theory is rigorous in its logic: As in all religious codes of law, for each crime there must be retribution. "Without blood there is no forgiveness" (Hebrews 9:22). In order for the soul's need for punishment to be satisfied effectively, everything concerning criminal justice must have a solemn and sacred character, suffusing the courts, the police, and the accused or convicted himself with the majesty of law. "Punishment must be an honor. It must not only wipe out the stigma of crime, but must be regarded as a supplementary form of education, compelling a higher devotion to the public good."[35]

Just as the musician awakens through sounds the ability to perceive beauty, so the system of criminal justice must awaken in the criminal, through suffering or even death, the ability to perceive justice. The mechanism by which such an operation is accomplished is indeed delicate. In order not to betray its subtlety I quote the passage at some length:

Men who are so estranged from the good that they seek to spread evil everywhere can only be reintegrated with the good by having harm inflicted upon them. This must be done until the completely innocent part of their soul awakens with the surprised cry "Why am I being hurt?" The innocent part of the criminal's soul must then be fed to make it grow until it becomes able to judge and condemn his past crimes and at last, by the help of grace, to forgive them. With this the punishment is completed; the criminal has been reintegrated with the good and should be publicly and solemnly reintegrated with society. That is what punishment is. Even capital punishment, although it excludes reintegration with society in the literal sense, should be the same thing. Punishment is solely a method of procuring pure good for men who do not desire it. The art of punishing is the art of awakening in the criminal, by pain or even death, the desire for pure good.[36]

It was in Marseilles in 1941 that Weil documented herself on the French judicial system. She frequently went to the Palais de Justice during that time to observe trials. Reacting bitterly to the treatment of the ignorant and oppressed in these courts of law, she wrote: "Nothing is more frightful than the spectacle, now so frequent, of an accused whose situation provides him with nothing to fall back upon but his own words, and who is incapable of arranging these words because of his social origin and lack of culture, as he stands broken down by guilt, affliction and fear, stammering before judges who are not listening and who interrupt him in tones of ostentatious refinement."[37]

The ideal Weilian theory of criminal justice rests on the general concept of supernatural justice, a concept that is basic to all of her ethical thought. Given the inevitable inequality of power and status in society, one must perceive justice from two points of view: the more powerful, or benefactor, and the weaker, or beneficiary. For the benefactor, supernatural justice consists of acting toward one less powerful as if he were his equal, while knowing he is in fact more powerful. For the benefactor's goodness is a result of his generosity. Neither rebellious nor fawning, the beneficiary's gratitude is just as noble as the benefactor's generosity, since one must be capable of such generosity in order to recognize it.

It is in the context of just such an understanding of supernatural justice that Weil's vision of a humanized criminal justice system is possible. "It is important that the whole organization of penal justice should be directed toward obtaining from the magistrates and their assistants the attention that is due from every man to any person who may be in his power and from the accused his consent to the punishment inflicted, a consent of which the innocent Christ has given us the perfect model."[38]

Rural Rootlessness

Rootlessness among peasants and farm workers in the countryside presents some of the same problems that Weil observed among factory workers. But each problem must be approached with the perspective of the conditions that distinguish rural life from urban industrial society. She first points out the profound jealousy and envy that have separated peasants and urban workers ever since the rise of the cities in the Middle Ages. Peasants had long felt inferior to citydwellers, and their feelings were only intensified by stereotypical images of the two groups conveyed by the prewar mass media: Weil mentions radio, motion pictures, and especially the big-city sophistication of magazines like *Marie-Claire* (the American equivalent being something along the lines of *McCall's*).

The need for roots in the countryside begins essentially with the thirst for landowning. For the peasant who tills the soil and depends on it for his livelihood, it is a deeply natural, almost sacred need. For this reason, Weil would favor abolishing (with a few exceptions) huge agribusiness operations with absentee owners. Instead she prefers that each family work its own modest tract of land. In cases where heavy, expensive equipment and large-scale cultivation are warranted, she suggests a cooperative endeavor in which individual families would continue to own and intensively cultivate their portions of the whole but would manage the large-scale aspects cooperatively and collectively.

Weil also emphasizes the necessity for making the teenaged farmboy's entrance into the world of work a memorable event that excites his imagination and ambition. She believes that there should be a solemn ritual of initiation into the adult world of farm labor in the early teens, preferably presided over by the Church, so as to integrate the rich scriptural emphasis on agricultural life into the youth's experiential contact with the earth. In the late teens she would have the state offer, cost-free, an exchange that would allow the youth to travel, study, and work in other rural areas, in order to avoid the deracinating effects of boredom in farm life. As with factory workers, it would be a revival of the old *Tour de France,* a feature of medieval guilds. Education's role in combating rootlessness would be equally as important among farm workers as with factory workers, but the nature of subject matter, preparation of teachers, and pedagogical philosophy would be tailored to the specific needs of rural working people.

Patriotism

Weil places her plan for the postwar reconstruction of France squarely within the context of her historical situation. Having been violently uprooted by the German invasion and occupation, France needed to think out her new beginnings with a view to profiting from her past experience. As with the whole of Europe, twentieth-century France stood bereft of all collectivities through which her people were to be kept in contact with the spiritual nourishment of the past, save one. Family, profession, and region had long ceased to function effectively as channels or vehicles of tradition. The lone remaining collectivity that might serve to strengthen a sense of roots was the state. Yet the notion of the state had undergone a profound transformation from the medieval idea of country or nation.

According to Weil, between the reigns of Charles V (thirteenth century) and Louis XIV (seventeenth century) the institution of legitimate monarchy became one of omnipotent despotism. Richelieu and Louis XIV had created a totalitarian state, personified in the Sun King, long before the concept of patriotism was redirected in 1789 from the king to the state itself. Thus, when the architects of the French Revolution spoke of the state, they were already uprooted intellectuals obsessed by the ideology of progress, a notion diametrically opposed to tradition. From 1789 on, the concept of patriotism in France had been based paradoxically not on love of the past but instead on the most violent rupture with the country's past. Postrevolutionary patriotism became tainted by the longstanding resentment built up among the people for the despotic state that was represented by the monarch. The state became an absolute value to which one owed absolute faithfulness (or more recently, in the consumer age, an unlimited good to be exploited or consumed). Such an attitude—expressed so tellingly in the slogan "My country, right or wrong"—is described by Weil as an idolatry without love, the height of sterility. She reminds her countrymen that France is a temporal, finite, mortal entity. Such sobering lucidity enables her to propose a "new patriotism."

The overweening pride and the glory of force that are celebrated in French literary heroes like Corneille's Rodrigue, Horace, and Polyeucte had no place in the patriotism of which Weil's contemporaries seemed to be in such dire need. The only legitimate patriotism, she holds, would be modeled first on Joan of Arc, who said she felt pity for the French realm, and ultimately on Christ, whose compassion for Jerusalem is so movingly portrayed in Matthew 23:37–38.

The love and faithfulness to one's country, felt in a compassionate rather than a prideful way, then, suggested a very different attitude toward the political dilemmas with which postwar reconstruction would be fraught. Weil believed a Frenchman could only feel proud of his country's colonial empire if his patriotism was the kind seen in Richelieu, Louis XIV, and Charles Maurras. The Christian inspiration and that of 1789 made true French patriotism incompatible with imperial conquest. "Every other nation might have had the right to carve out an empire for itself, but not France; for the same reason which made the temporal sovereignty of the Pope a scandal in the eyes of Christendom. When one takes upon oneself, as France did in 1789, the function of thinking on behalf of the world, of defining justice for the world, one may not become an owner of human flesh and blood."[39]

It is squarely in this line of thinking that Weil offers a rather novel interpretation of Charles Péguy's patriotism. She finds Péguy's admiration for the Roman Empire quite inconsistent with his opposition to the Germans, who in World War I were trying to duplicate the accomplishments of the Roman Empire and by the same brutal methods. Whereas this contradiction did not keep Péguy from dying for France in the War of 1914, it is, she believes, precisely what kept many French youth in 1940 from imitating him, even though they acted in the same spirit. Bernanos, on the other hand, with the advantage of another generation's history behind him, clearly understood and declared that Hitler's Germany was a return to pagan Rome.

Weil was, as one might expect, an admirer of Gandhi's pacifism, although she said it had never been strictly applied, even by Gandhi himself, who was too practical-minded for that. Rather than being in conflict with patriotism, Weil saw radical pacifism as a way of being patriotic. She tried to envision what it would have been like in 1940 if France had been able to apply the principle in all its radical selflessness. Passive resistance to the occupation forces would certainly have caused many more Frenchmen to die for their country, undoubtedly in horrifying circumstances. It would have amounted to "an imitation of Christ's passion realized on a national scale."[40] Yet civil disobedience was, for Weil, a legitimate course of action only in relatively unusual cases. "If one feels inclined to disobey, but one is dissuaded by the excessive danger involved, that is altogether unpardonable, whether it be because one contemplated an act of disobedience, or else because one failed to carry it out, as the case may be. Besides, whenever one isn't strictly obliged to disobey, one is under the strict obligation to obey. . . . Public order ought to be regarded as more sacred than private property."[41]

During a time of grave national emergency when the very survival of one's country hangs in the balance, it is no easy task to retain objectivity in analyzing political, social, and moral issues. That Weil was so often able to achieve this and never shrank from voicing unpopular views is one more testimony to the prophetic nature of her writing. Although she was devoted to the Free French movement to the point of earnestly wishing to die serving its aims, she had no illusions about the fallibility of her compatriots and the enormous challenge they would face in the event of an Allied victory. France in 1943, she pointed out, happened to be defending all the right causes, but the affliction she was combating had made it all too easy to be unified on the right side of justice. Once the Allies defeated the Nazis, France would be thrust again into the real world where right and wrong are more complicated.

Even in the dilemma of living in Occupied France, Weil saw more than a cut-and-dried choice of good and evil. When she arrived in the United States in 1942, she was offended by those who assumed all Vichy sympathizers were traitors and all resisters were saints. "There was once a nation which believed itself to be holy, with the direst consequences for its well-being; and in connection with this, it is strange indeed to reflect that the Pharisees were the resisters in this nation, and the publicans the collaborators, and then to remind oneself what were Christ's relations with each of these two national groups."[42] To make the situation of collaborators more easily understood, Weil compares them to other assimilated peoples of history. They would stand in relation to an eventual Europe of a hypothetical German victory in much the same position as, say, Provençal, Breton, or Alsatian people are expected to stand in relation to the French government today.

The demands of the wartime situation on the French moral character had taken their toll. Weil remarked that an Allied victory would liberate a country full of people who had been conditioned to disobey. Distributing forbidden literature, black-marketing, intentionally working poorly at various jobs had once been considered laudable in the cause of the Resistance. Once liberated, these same people would be expected to turn immediately to practicing obedience. Having undergone protracted periods of rationing and deprivation, they would look forward to indulging their long-denied dreams of eating their fill. A beggar's attitude toward the state would become all the more ingrained in the national consciousness. A diffused terrorism caused by widely encouraging the dream to kill, even though invoking the highest motive, would need to be tamed without recourse to the repressive police state. In short, "the government which arises in France after the liberation of the country will have to face a triple danger caused by this blood lust, this mendicity complex, and this inability to obey."[43]

Pacifism and Resistance

Weil's strong sympathy with the cause of pacifism left her no illusions about the purity of motives among many pacifists. She believed there should be a wartime service option for conscientious objectors that would be more arduous and perilous than military service, in order to weed out those who rationalize their status for the wrong reasons. A project such as her own front-line emergency nursing squad might well have served this purpose. According to Weil, conscientious objectors act out of two distinct motives: an aversion to killing and an aversion to being killed. The dishonor of refusing to defend one's country should be punished by exile rather than imprisonment; the latter punishment she finds shocking because it puts draft evasion on the same level with theft and murder. Military duty, furthermore, must not depend on how well the country fulfills its purpose of conveying the spiritual nourishment called rootedness. The degree to which a country so functions may always be enhanced, whereas the destruction of one's country renders rootedness a virtual impossibility. An enlightening historical judgment on this subject is Weil's analysis of the French pacifists in World War I. Their mistake, she holds, was to have appealed to the baser motives of security and comfort in order to gain a broader base of political power. Their error had the damaging effect of dishonoring true devotion to peace.

Despite the worldwide prestige enjoyed by France after 1789 as the cradle of liberty, equality, and fraternity, the French state had fallen progressively, Weil believed, throughout the nineteenth century, culminating in the disaster of 1940, to the level of other Western states, namely, that of proud imperial conqueror of peoples. The dashing of that dream of conquest and false grandeur in 1940, she concluded, had given France the opportunity to reassume her role as model of justice among the nations. The Free French movement was not only a means of liberation but an inspirational example of devotion to justice. "The French movement in London has precisely the necessary degree of official character for its directives to have the force of orders, but without diminishing the kind of lucid and pure rapture that goes with free acceptance of sacrifice. Its possibilities and its responsibilities are, therefore, immense."[44] The new French republic should be patterned, she thought, after groups that were spontaneously growing up all over France and putting

into action the words of inspiration they were hearing from London.
But this patterning process, according to Weil, had to begin immediately, before the Allied victory set off the inevitable feverish
pursuit of individual well-being and power that would characterize
postliberation France. "Four obstacles above all separate us from a
civilization likely to be worth something: our false conception of
greatness; the degradation of the sentiment of justice; our idolization
of money; and our lack of religious inspiration."[45]

Mystique of Work

"The spiritual function of physical labor is the contemplation of
things, the contemplation of nature."[46] Simone Weil's mystique of
work is at the heart of her philosophy. It underlies her own existential
involvement among working-class people and it shapes her sociopolitical thought throughout. To contemplate nature is to comprehend the reign of the order of necessity, to learn the perfect obedience
of inanimate creation to the world order ordained by God. It is an
apprenticeship in the Stoic lessons of anonymity and of de-creation.

Weil's life may best be understood in terms of her death—a
voluntary sacrifice of her self (her energy, her time, her "attention")
to the reign of necessity or gravity. "Physical labor is a daily death."[47]
"Physical labor willingly consented to is, after death willingly consented to, the most perfect form of obedience."[48] The theological basis for such an understanding of work lies in the biblical
account of Adam and Eve's expulsion from the garden.
The free choice of man not to obey brought on God's punishment
in the form of death and labor. In the context of Weil's above-
described philosophy of crime and punishment, then, it is admirably
logical that "labor and death, if Man undergoes them in a spirit of
willingness, constitute a transference back into the current of supreme good, which is obedience to God."[49]

The quintessential thrust of Simone Weil's entire career—both
her life and her writings—has to do with this highly illuminating
vision of the mystique of work. It is not surprising to find an
eloquent formulation of the vision at the end of L'Enracinement. It
sums up, in fact, the whole book and the whole significance of
Weil's sociopolitical philosophy. "It is not difficult to define the
place that physical labor should occupy in a well-ordered social life.
It should be its spiritual core."[50]

In "Le Christianisme et la vie des champs" (Christianity and farm life) Weil makes an eloquent argument for the sacred character of work. "Manual labor is either a degrading servitude for the soul or a sacrifice. In the case of working in the fields, the link with the Eucharist, if only it is felt, is sufficient to make of it a sacrifice."[51] Beginning with agricultural life, she recalls the innumerable comparisons in Jesus' teachings between the life of the spirit and the daily life of the planter and husbandman. The comparisons are extended to all professions and trades in her philosophy, but particularly in manual labor. The manual laborer, whether on the farm or in the factory, burns or consumes his flesh and transforms it into energy as a machine burns fuel. He thus gives his body and his blood to be transformed into the fruits of his labor (crops, livestock, manufactured goods). In each trade, Weil identifies the relation to the Gospel in this rich biblical anagoge of work. "What is needed is . . . to find and define for each aspect of social life its specific link with Christ. . . . Thus, as religious life is distributed in orders corresponding to vocations, so in like manner would social life appear as an edifice of distinct vocations converging in Christ."[52] "It is a question of transforming, in the largest possible measure, daily life itself into a metaphor with a divine significance, a parable."[53]

Chapter Four
Ways to the Divine: Beauty
The True, the Good, the Beautiful

Near the beginning of this study I wrote that Simone Weil's thought is holistic and that it is, therefore, rather misleading to compartmentalize her philosophy under convenient and familiar rubrics. That statement applies particularly well to her thinking on beauty and knowledge. Her aesthetics, criticism, philosophy of education, and philosophy of science are all components of the central vision of truth and of God that is the fountainhead of Weil's wisdom. For these reasons I have chosen to give the same general title to chapters 4 and 5, consciously seeking to emphasize their intimate interrelatedness. Beauty and knowledge are not only two of the universals—along with the good—of Platonic philosophy that illuminate the seeker's "way to the divine." They often appear to be almost indistinguishable in Weil's philosophy. "There exists a focal point of greatness where the genius creating beauty, the genius revealing truth, heroism, and holiness are indistinguishable."[1] Not only does she agree with Keats's "Ode on a Grecian Urn" about the identification of truth and beauty; she places the artist, the sage, the hero, and the saint together in the same lofty region of "genius," all drawing their worth and talent from the supreme source of the good. They are all prophets. The hero and the saint are those who are favored with the divine election to receive affliction, to suffer for their God or for their earthly community (e.g., Prometheus, Antigone, Christ). The artist and the sage are contemplatives. Through their eyes others are enabled to perceive more clearly the beauty and symmetry of the world order, and, therefore, the meaning of the suffering experienced willingly by the hero and the saint. "The artist, the scholar, the philosopher, the contemplative should really admire the world and pierce through the film of unreality that veils it and makes of it, for nearly all men at nearly every moment of their lives, a dream or stage set."[2]

Simone Weil's aesthetics takes its origin in her metaphysical vision and never strays far from it. The basis for all her ideas on beauty, on art, and on the artist is to be found in a line of thinking that she expresses perhaps best in *Attente de Dieu*. In the all-important essay on "Love of the Order of the World" she notes that there is very little mention in the Gospel of the beauty of the world, aside from isolated passages such as those on the lilies of the field, arrayed in more splendor than Solomon, and the birds of the air, which take no thought for the future. The latter example, and that of God sending the rain on the just as well as the unjust, show that the idea of beauty is closely associated in Weil's mind with the beauty of the world order. Therefore, the artist's contemplation of beauty is intimately related to the Stoic love of necessity or *amor fati*. "Beauty is necessity which, while remaining in conformity with its own law and with that alone, is obedient to the good."[3]

The key insight in this meditation is that beauty is a means. It points our way to God. Our contemplation of beauty must never stop with the particular thing of beauty (whether it be a landscape, a work of art, or an occurrence). Instead, we must allow the object to lead us beyond itself, and, ultimately, to the beautiful, because for Weil the beautiful is also the true and the good, or God. "The great sorrow of human life is that looking and eating are two different operations."[4] All sin, she declares, is an attempt to consume, to "eat" beauty, that is, to consume what should only be looked at and used as a means, a *metaxu*. The archetype of all sin is Eve in the garden. If, once placed in Eve's situation, we can look at the fruit without eating it, if we can consider the thing of beauty purely as a means to lead us to God, then art becomes redemptive. "The attitude of looking and waiting is the attitude which corresponds with the beautiful."[5]

In "Human Personality," Weil probes the nature of the beautiful, demonstrating in an illuminating passage the inevitable dead end of such experiments as those of Rimbaud and the Surrealists, who looked to the beautiful as the all-sufficient source and as the object of their worship.

Beauty is the supreme mystery of this world. It is a gleam which attracts the attention and yet does nothing to sustain it. Beauty always promises, but never gives anything; it stimulates hunger but has no nourishment for the part of the soul which looks in this world for sustenance. It feeds only the part of the soul that gazes. While exciting desire, it makes clear that there is nothing in it to be desired, because the one thing we want is that it should not change. If one does not seek means to evade the exquisite anguish it inflicts, then desire is gradually transformed into love; and one begins to acquire the faculty of pure and disinterested attention.[6]

Here Weil analyzes with great clarity the roots of the cult of beauty that persisted in France from Baudelaire and Art for Art's Sake through its metamorphosis into the ideal of *le merveilleux* among the Dadaists and Surrealists. She takes it as a point of departure for a modern reworking of the Platonic doctrine of beauty as perceived through the filter of the cross.

Malheur in Art

For Weil, art is the result of an experience of suffering, and its enjoyment is an analogous experience. It is a discipline of the soul in both cases. Wherever there is beauty, there is pain, both in its origin and in its perpetuation. We are to "feast our eyes," as the saying goes in English, but our eyes in this case symbolize the part of the soul that looks on, not the part that consumes. Whenever Weil mentions a "beautiful" work of literature—be it *Phèdre, King Lear, The Iliad,* or the Book of Job—she has in mind an intimate link to the archetypal story of redemptive suffering recorded in the Gospels: the Passion of Jesus Christ. Alfred de Musset and the other Romantic poets were known for their "Pelicanism," a doctrine that urged the poet to sing of his personal grief. "Ta douleur est à Dieu" (Thy grief is divine), says the muse to the poet in Musset's *La Nuit de Mai.* But whereas the Romantics too often used this doctrine as a pretext to vent themselves of shallow, even puerile sentimentality, the role of suffering in art takes on an infinitely deeper significance in Weil's aesthetics. "The radiance of beauty illumines affliction with the light of the spirit of justice and love, which is the only light by which human thought can confront affliction and report the truth of it."[7]

Weil sees the very essence of beauty in the suffering, grief, and affliction of the cross, and perhaps most eloquently in Christ's lament: "My God, My God, why hast Thou forsaken Me?"

God . . . created beings capable of love from all possible distances. Because no other could do it, he himself went to the greatest possible distance, the infinite distance. This infinite distance between God and God, this supreme tearing apart, this agony beyond all others, this marvel of love, is the crucifixion. Nothing can be further from God than that which has been made accursed. This tearing apart, over which supreme love places the bond of supreme union, echoes perpetually across the universe in the midst of the silence, like two notes, separate yet melting into one, like pure and heart-rending harmony. This is the Word of God. The whole creation is nothing but its vibration. When human music in its greatest purity pierces our soul, this is what we hear through it. When we have learned to hear the silence, this is what we grasp more distinctly through it.[8]

The supreme importance of suffering in the beautiful work of art and its redemptive nature help explain how Weil came to believe that a truly great text, such as *Antigone* or *The Iliad,* could be understood equally well by factory workers and by the more highly educated elite. It also sheds light on the powerful spiritual influence exerted on Weil by ostensibly aesthetic experiences such as the recitation of Herbert's poem "Love" and the Greek text of the Lord's Prayer, as well as the Gregorian plainchant that she heard at Solesmes during Holy Week in 1938. Life and art can never be divorced one from the other, she clearly implies. Literature is not the pastime of effete snobs. It grows out of, and therefore expresses, man's deepest responses to the social, political, psychological, and spiritual dilemmas of his experience.

Here, as in other instances, it is instructive to compare Weil's thought to that of Albert Camus. The great philosopher-artist of the absurd, who had a profound admiration for Weil's work, declared in his Stockholm address in 1957 that the artist could never again allow himself to remain disengaged from the great sociopolitical issues of his time, that he was irrevocably thrust into the arena. Weil no doubt would have stated the problem differently. Perhaps she would have said the artist proceeds from the arena, thus rendering moot the question of taking sides on particular issues. The Weilian artist, rather than engaging in polemics, reveals human problems in their deep complexities, shedding the light of wisdom on them in the ongoing quest for transcendent truth. What she and Camus would certainly have agreed upon, however, is that true artistic beauty is the product of a living, often painful contact with the real world of human experience, rather than an ethereal pursuit of aesthetic values (the perfection of form in Art for Art's Sake) or an artificial surreality *(le merveilleux).* The scorn for the utility of art in Gautier and Leconte de Lisle, as well as in Breton's Surrealist manifestos, had the effect of setting up the artist as a priest in the cult of art, a cult that was to take precedence over all other values. In the hands of these writers, Victor Hugo's poet-priest evolved, in the half-century following his death, into an omnipotent seer engaged in a Rimbaudian quest for a new order. But Rimbaud's example showed the dead end of such a quest. Weil believed, with Dostoyevski, that beauty could save the world. But the word beauty, both for her and for the creator of Ivan Karamazov, had a much richer and more fully human meaning.

It was for these reasons that Weil included certain artists on her list of scientists, scholars, and political figures who shared aspirations to what she called "false greatness" *(la fausse grandeur).* One may write lines that will enable one to live on in the world's memory by the sheer greatness of their form. But if there is no substance contained therein, the writer has only attained a false form of greatness rather than true genius.

Works of art that are neither pure and true reflections of the beauty of the world nor openings onto this beauty are not strictly speaking beautiful; their authors may be very talented but they lack real genius. That is true of a great many works of art which are among the most celebrated and the most highly praised. Every true artist has had real, direct, and immediate contact with the beauty of the world, contact that is of the nature of a sacrament. God has inspired every first-rate work of art, though its subject may be utterly and entirely secular; he has not inspired any of the others. Indeed the luster of beauty that distinguishes some of those others may quite well be a diabolical luster.[9]

"God has inspired every first-rate work of art; . . . he has not inspired any of the others." That is a far-reaching statement both about the nature of aesthetic quality and about religious art. For Weil, all truly great art is religious in that it partakes of the beautiful, which cannot be divorced from the good. "One cannot reach the good without passing through the beautiful,"[10] and the converse would hold true as well. Artistic beauty is a reflection of the beauty of the reign of impersonal necessity in the artist, whose personality is only an instrument and not the focal point. If one objects that some of Weil's favorite artists were anything but Christian, her reply is that even the unbelieving artist, when he reaches the heights of genius, is unconsciously obedient to God's inspiration. "In everything which gives us the pure authentic feeling of beauty there is really the presence of God . . . Contact with the beautiful is a sacrament in the full sense of the word."[11]

Nature and Imitation

One of the aesthetic doctrines that have been often and widely repeated is the notion that an artist is great insofar as he exerts his will upon the raw material of nature and obliges it to take whatever form he chooses. In Weil's aesthetics, however, nature is never beautiful when it obeys man, only when it obeys God. "If sometimes a work of art seems almost as beautiful as the sea, the mountains, or flowers, it is because the light of God has filled the artist."[12] Thus, the role of the artist takes on a more passive character; he is a vessel, an instrument in the hands of the Almighty. Weil often expresses in her notebooks the aspiration to become perfectly obedient to God, "like a pencil pushed across the paper by me."[13] The great artist is like a pencil in the hand of the divine poet.

Similarly, Weil gives a new interpretation to the traditional aesthetic teaching that the artist imitates God. It is not in his creative power that he resembles the Creator but in a kind of self-abnegation. The beauty of his work reflects the beauty of the world order, and the rules of rhyme and versification in art are equivalent to the reign of necessity in nature. A word is found in a poem in a given position because it belongs there and because the poet is obedient to the inspiration of the beautiful, not because of a specific preoccupation with rhyme, rhythm, or grammar. "If an artist tries to imitate either some sense object or some psychological phenomenon, such as feeling, etc., his work is mediocre. In creating a work of art of the highest class the artist's attention is oriented towards silence and the void; from this silence and void there descends an inspiration which develops into words or forms. . . . (There is no particular intention in art. The poet who puts in a certain particular word for a certain particular effect is a mediocre poet.)"[14]

Overeager exponents of textual analysis are mistaken when they presume to explain the presence of a word or phrase in a poem by the poet's desire to obtain a given effect. Such presumptuous practitioners of *explication de texte* are compared by Weil to believers who see the providential hand of God only in the more notably beneficent

occurrences of life. The apprenticeship of the believer is to enable
him increasingly to see in absolutely every occurrence the obedience
of the world to the reign of necessity and to the perfect will of the
Father. And analogously, in a fragment that has attained to the
perfection of poetic beauty, says Weil, "all the effects, all the res-
onances, all the evocatory qualities capable of being summoned
together by the presence of a word in such-and-such a place correspond in an equal degree, that is to say, perfectly, to the poet's
inspiration. It is the same with all the arts. It is in this way that
the poet imitates God."[15]

Time and Space

Simone Weil was clearly a firm believer in the importance of
discipline, and one of the disciplines she practiced most religiously
was that of time and the temporal order. To remind oneself constantly of the limitations of the human condition, and above all of
time and space, was to submit oneself more perfectly to the reign
of necessity in the world order. Hence the importance of manual
labor as a spiritual exercise. So in Weil's aesthetics it should be no
surprise to discover that the whole purpose of art is "to make us
feel space and time. To fabricate for us a human space and time,
made by man, which nevertheless is true time and true space."[16] A
painting, she says, is a finite space fixed within the boundaries of
a frame, but in which there must also be the infinite. Similarly,
what she calls "perfect poems" are those that have a beginning and
an end, a duration that is an image of eternity in human time.
Great art, like great philosophy, makes us more aware of reality.
"Art is an attempt to transport into a limited quantity of matter,
modeled by man, an image of the infinite beauty of the entire
universe. If the attempt succeeds, this portion of matter should not
hide the universe, but on the contrary it should reveal its reality to
all around."[17] "The violence of time lacerates the soul; through that
laceration enters eternity."[18]

Love in Art

Some of the most profound philosophical and religious texts in
world literature were written in the language of love: the Song of
Solomon, Dante's *Divine Comedy*, Boethius's *Consolation of Philosophy*.
It is in such a tradition that one should place Weil when she writes

that mystics should not be criticized for using the language of love. They are precisely the ones who most legitimately use it, she insists, and others may only borrow it for more vulgar uses. For carnal love in all its forms is at bottom only a thinly masked quest for the beauty of the world order. Francesca seems only interested in possessing Paolo physically in the *Inferno*, and Emma Bovary's desire for Rodolphe appears limited to a rather base instinct. "But it is all the beauty of the world, it is universal beauty, for which we yearn. This kind of transference is what all love literature expresses, from the most ancient and well-worn metaphors and comparisons to the subtle analyses of Proust. The longing to love the beauty of the world in a human being is essentially the longing for the Incarnation."[19] It is an understanding of love that is akin to the picture drawn by Mauriac in *Le Désert de l'amour* (*The Desert of Love*, 1925): "Il n'y a qu'un seul amour" ("There is but one love"). Between the lines of all love stories, she implies, there is an ever-present paradigm: the age-old quest of the Messiah for his bride.

Art and Morality

Mauriac, Maritain, Julien Green, and other modern French writers have inaugurated an ongoing discussion of the true relation of art to one's moral convictions, especially in the context of the Christian faith. They all seem convinced, as are so many modern writers, that art is inevitably bound up with evil. Some have contended that narrative fiction, in particular, is impossible without the "raw material" of evil that it uses in the creative process. Simone Weil agrees that fiction, of necessity, deals in evil more extensively than in good. Her own explanation of this apparent law of literature is that in real life evil is "dreary, monotonous, and boring" and good is "beautiful . . . wonderful . . . fresh and surprising"; whereas in fiction the opposite holds true. "Fictional good is boring and flat, while fictional evil is varied and intriguing, attractive, profound, and full of charm."[20]

Consequently, fiction has an inherent tendency toward immorality. In writers of true genius, according to Weil, the fictional world presented to the reader actually transcends the order of fiction that is bound to evil. They give us "in the guise of fiction something equivalent to the actual density of the real" because they are "outside the realm of fiction and they release us from it."[21] This heightened sense of the real that is portrayed in truly great fiction is the most moral of literary modes, whereas mediocre fiction is irrevocably bound to evil. Thus, Weil holds that a writer should never be accused of immorality. Such a condemnation should actually be directed at his lack of genius. She implies that the intensity of the discussion over art and morality in the twentieth century has a great deal to do with the growing modern tendency of the public to look upon writers in general as spiritual guides. Most writers are entirely incapable of performing that function, and those who would arrogate it to themselves are guilty of a "Messianic delusion." We may be legitimately guided, she maintains, by the works of true genius from the past, for, as Plato said, they are able to "make us grow wings to overcome gravity."[22]

The writers guilty of the Messianic delusion were typified for Weil in the generation between the two wars, in which many openly claimed the function of director of conscience. André Gide, for example, could not have been unaware that books like *Les Nourritures Terrestres* (*Fruits of the Earth*, 1897) and *Les Caves du Vatican* (*Lafcadio's Adventures*, 1914) would have a great influence on men's actions. Yet he and others refused to be held responsible for such influences and insisted upon the absolute freedom of the artist, retreating "behind the sacred privilege of art for art's sake. . . . There, then, is no reason for placing such books behind the inviolable barrier of art for art's sake, and sending to prison a young fellow who pushes somebody off a train in motion."[23] "One might just as well claim the privileges of art for art's sake in support of crime. At one time the Surrealists came pretty close to doing so."[24] Weil insists that it is absurd to exclude literature from questions of moral good and evil "since readers are not a separate animal species and since people who read are the same ones who perform a great many other functions."[25]

Weil sees the dominant characteristic of literature in the first half of the twentieth century as the loss of the idea of value. Bergson's concept of life force (*l'élan vital*) is value-free; Surrealism is the "intoxication of total license . . . a clean sweep of value and surrender to the immediate . . . the literary equivalent for the sacking of towns"[26] and Proust is concerned with analyzing "non-oriented states of soul."[27] The latter illustrates Weil's conviction that twentieth-century literature in general is essentially psychological, since psychology, too, is concerned with describing states of soul without reference to moral good or evil, that is, in a value-free domain.

Weil calls Rimbaud the epitome of demoniacal genius. She explains the ultimate failure of Rimbaud's poetic revolt in these terms: "Since the maturity of genius is conformity to the true relations of good and evil, the work which represents maturity of demoniacal genius is silence."[28] She declares that it is inaccurate to interpret Rimbaud and the Dadaists and Surrealists as literary heirs of Villon. The crimes of Villon were committed out of necessity or weakness, not as a thrill or a gratuitous act, and the proper relation of moral good and evil is preeminently clear thoughout Villon's poetry.

Weil's Criticism of the *Iliad*

It is often true that the most brilliant interpretations of literature come not from the literary critics themselves but rather from the great poets, philosophers, and artists who have reflected on others' works: Eliot on Dante, Sartre on Genet, Nietzsche on Greek tragedy, and Baudelaire on nineteenth-century French painting. Simone Weil never wrote anything purely as a literary critic. Yet she often made judgments of literary and artistic quality, as may be clearly seen in the above consideration of her aesthetic thought. Not surprisingly, her judgments are usually moral as much as aesthetic in nature, but she also sometimes betrays a remarkable clarity of insight into the workings of literary and artistic genius. Most of her criticisms are scattered throughout her philosophical writings, forming a wealth of *exempla* that she draws upon in order to illustrate a point in her moral philosophy or her speculative reasoning. The only text she devoted entirely to a literary work was the essay written in 1940 and entitled *"L'Iliade, ou le poème de la Force."*[29] Even there, the focus of inquiry is far broader than that of a close reading of the text. What the "critic" is really after is something much greater than the meaning of the specific text in question or the way its author succeeded in giving it such staying power. Instead, she uses Homer's poem as the pretext for a philosophical meditation, but a philosophical meditation that illumines not only the broad human problems of violence, force, and justice but also the very nature of artistic vision in works of true genius. Such a procedure probably grew out of Weil's teaching method. In her philosophy classes she preferred to use the texts of the great literary giants for discussion rather than strictly philosophical texts.

Weil sees the greatness of the *Iliad* in the extraordinary equity or fairness that informs Homer's treatment of the themes of violence and force. Force, she says, is the only hero of the *Iliad,* its true center and its true subject. She defines force as that which transforms whatever it touches into an object, a thing. Force, power, and violence here are all manifestations of "gravity," as she defined it in *La Pesanteur et la grâce.* Force is the image of our common mortality: "Exercised to the limit, it turns man into a thing in the most literal sense: it makes a corpse out of him."[30]

The genius of the *Iliad* lies in its graphic demonstration of the laws of necessity as they emerge in a clear vision of war. Those who find themselves in possession of force tend to think of it as absolute, although that is impossible. They are unconscious of the limits of power. "Thus it happens that those who have force on loan from fate count on it too much and are destroyed."[31] No one is excepted from submission to a superior force in the *Iliad,* neither Greek nor Trojan. Even Achilles suffers a public humiliation at the hands of Agamemnon in the opening scene, and he cringes with fear before the raging river. Furthermore, it is not only the victims of force that suffer its dehumanizing effects. Those who wield it are intoxicated by it. "Violence obliterates anybody who feels its touch. It comes to seem just as external to its employer as to its victim. And from this springs the idea of destiny before which executioner and victim stand equally innocent, before which conquered and conqueror are brothers in the same distress."[32]

Since all come under the sway of force in the *Iliad* and since both conqueror and conquered alike are victimized by the dehumanizing touch of violence, the poem is an admirable portrayal of the Stoic laws of necessity that govern the affairs of earth. It is not the heroic deeds of great warriors that precipitate the drama so much as blind necessity or fate, symbolized by the golden scales of Zeus. This impersonal reign of necessity, whose blows are felt with equal grief for Greeks and Trojans, is the world order that Weil and the Stoics would have us accept, and even embrace willingly. It touches once again upon the genius for suffering that is at the heart of Weil's philosophical message. "This retribution [*châtiment*], which has a geometrical rigor, which operates automatically to penalize the abuse of force, was the main subject of Greek thought."[33] Weil believed this same geometrically rigorous law of necessity was the soul of the Greek epic, the mainspring of Greek tragedy (Nemesis), and the point of departure for all Greek wisdom concerning the nature of man and the universe. She sees the same notion in the Buddhist doctrine of Kharma: a sense of limit, measure, balance, the kind of idea that has been almost obliterated from the modern Western mind. "We are only geometricians of matter; the Greeks were, first of all, geometricians in their apprenticeship to virtue."[34]

The absolute sway of necessity, the ineluctable reign of force in the *Iliad* not only has the effect of creating an admirable equity. It also has the potential of painting a rather dismal, monotonous atmosphere of horror and suffering. Such a danger is averted, according to Weil, by the occasional presence of "those few luminous moments, scattered here and there throughout the poem, those brief, celestial moments in which man possesses his soul."[35] Hector's courage in the face of certain death, scenes of or allusions to conjugal and filial love, and the tradition of hospitality are examples of how Homer has preserved fragile human tenderness and affection in this story of cruel force. But the greatest example of the triumph of love's purity in the midst of battle is "the friendship that floods the hearts of mortal enemies. . . . Before it . . . the distance between benefactor and suppliant, between victor and vanquished, shrinks to nothing. . . . These moments of grace are rare in the *Iliad,* but they are enough to make us feel with sharp regret what it is that violence has killed and will kill again."[36]

Weil sees the *Iliad* as the West's only authentic epic, essentially because of the unusual equity with which it presents war, the ultimate experience of force. The *Odyssey* and the *Aeneid,* she declares, are "excellent imitations" at best, the latter tainted by "frigidity, bombast, and bad taste." The *Chanson de Roland* and other *chansons de geste* are conspicuously lacking in that equity Weil so admires in the *Iliad.* The deaths of heathens are not felt with any sadness or sympathy compared to the description of Roland's death. The true continuation of the epic spirit, according to Weil, is found in the tragedies of Aeschylus and Sophocles and the crowning achievements of Greek culture, the Gospels.

Random Critical Commentaries

Most of Simone Weil's critical judgments on art and literature occur incidentally in essays and letters that focus principally on other matters. Her experimental method of thinking on paper was thus enhanced by the applications of the philosophical principles in question to the less speculative domain of the artist's created universe. And by the same token, the broader implications of the artistic creation that she used for such purposes were often illuminated in a compelling insight.

A prime example of these random critical judgments is a note on Proust that is found in "God in Plato." The context is a brilliant meditation on the Platonic conception of memory. Since all men experienced, before life on earth as we know it, a direct and clear contemplation of the transcendent realities (the true, the good, the beautiful) in a celestial state, the secret of spiritual experience in earthly life has to do with memory. Even recalling our earthly past has a near-sacred character: this truth is reflected in the central role of remembering in such sacraments as the Eucharist. "Our thoughts are by nature limited to the realities of this world. The past is a reality which is on our level, but it is absolutely beyond our reach. We cannot take a single step towards it but can only orient our minds so as to receive an emanation from it. It is for this reason that the past is the best image of the eternal, supernatural realities. (The joy and the beauty of remembering is perhaps connected with this.) Proust had a glimpse of it."[37]

One of the more devastating factors in the process of deracination of modern society, according to Weil, is the tragic loss of the collective past. The technological advances of travel and communication, which tended to minimize traditional regional distinctiveness, were instrumental in progressively obliterating the quaint old ways of the rural past. It was for these reasons that she found a particular value in George Sand, who preserved in her writings some of the ancient customs of her native Berry province.

Weil's judgments tend to fall under the two categories of bitter denunciations and soaring encomiums. The intensity of approval or disapproval doubtless grew out of a conviction that literature was much more than a game or a diversion. To her it was a part of the great battle for the mind and the spirit. She drew rather sharp lines between good art and bad, and usually her rationale for such judgments was clearly delineated.

One of the great names of classical French literature that suffered frequent attacks at Weil's hands was Pierre Corneille, one of the trio of giants (with Racine and Molière) of the French theater during its moment of triumph, the seventeenth century. First, Weil could not forgive him for the dedications of his plays addressed to Richelieu in what she finds base, servile language. Considering Weil's opinion of Richelieu, creator of the modern French omnipotent and autonomous state, one is hardly surprised by the criticism, even though it actually concerns Corneille's extraliterary activity rather than the literary quality of the plays themselves. But in the dramatic texts, too, Weil finds a reflection of the same attitudes. She concludes that Corneille was right to dedicate *Horace* to Richelieu because the "almost delirious pride that permeates this tragedy" goes hand in hand with the baseness of the dedication. The inseparability of this baseness and pride is demonstrated, she says, in Nazi Germany. She finds Polyeucte guilty of setting out to conquer the spiritual realm that he has just discovered with the same attitude and methods he formerly used as an imperial Roman soldier. The concluding statement is one of the more striking of Weil's critical aphorisms: "Alexander wept, we are told, because he had only the terrestrial globe to conquer. Corneille apparently thought Christ had come down to earth to make up for this deficiency."[38]

The same kind of vile servility Weil saw in Corneille's dedicatory prefaces was characteristic, she believed, of a great part of seventeenth-century France, as one may easily perceive in the memoirs of Saint-Simon. Molière, she remarks, did not evidently write *Le Misanthrope* as a simple entertainment, but also as a social document of the times. Bossuet was for her too obviously symbolic of the Church's servile attitude toward the state to be admirable. And he subscribed to the providential conception of history as well. Such an interpretation of history Weil termed "appalling and stupid, equally revolting for the intelligence as for the heart. One has to be more than ordinarily sensitive to the resonance of words to be able to regard this courtier-prelate as a great mind."[39] In Italian literature's hall of fame the venality of Ariosto, displayed so blatantly in his dedicatory preface to his patron, the Duke of Este, automatically consigns him to the ranks of the despicable in Weil's judgment.

All of the above condemnations have to do with what Weil calls the second Renaissance, the revival of the Roman spirit and culture, as opposed to the Hellenistic early Renaissance. The Roman admiration of conquest and brute force, the Roman notion of political rights as opposed to moral obligations, and the Roman belief in their providential destiny to reign supreme, according to Weil, were the seeds of corruption in the second Renaissance and the Roman

Catholic Church. Her occasional attacks on Jacques Maritain, too, are related to the same objections. However, one wonders whether Weil was familiar with the Maritain of *Humanisme intégral* (*Integral Humanism*) and *Primauté du spirituel* (*The Things That Are Not Caesar's*). This Maritain, after all, had repudiated Maurras's Action Française movement and his philosophy of "politics first." Weil may simply have been unable to forgive Maritain, not only for his link to the reactionary Maurras but also for his veneration of Aquinas and Aristotle over Plato.

Weil's Pantheon of True Genius

From the critical judgments of Simone Weil it is clear by now that she reckoned as beautiful that which seemed eminently true and that beauty, on the other hand, was for her the sign and seal of truth as well. Speaking of Saint John of the Cross, she declares: "The beauty of his writings is a sufficiently clear indication of their authenticity."[40] Near the end of *L'Enracinement*, she gives a partial list of her favorite artists, a kind of Pantheon of those who represent for her the dazzling truth and beauty of pure genius. The persuasiveness of her argument is weakened when she appears intent on proclaiming each of these geniuses a saint: it is spurious reasoning to hold that artistic genius is a sure indication of spiritual worth. One may understand her observation that the spirit of mystical illumination is all but inseparable from artistic genius in Giotto, in the Zen poets and painters of China, and in Velasquez. But it is difficult to go so far as to agree that "the *Iliad*, the tragedies of Aeschylus and those of Sophocles bear the clearest indication that the poets who produced them were in a state of holiness," or that "Monteverdi, Bach, Mozart were beings whose lives were pure even as were their works."[41] The proof text that she cites is Jesus' statement that a good tree produces good fruit and a corrupt tree, bad fruit, that "you will know them by their fruits" (Matthew 7:16–17). The "fruits" of this verse must certainly refer, however, to moral acts, not works of art. Nevertheless, the listing of Weil's Pantheon is an interesting selection and tells a great deal about her aesthetics and criticism.

Weil first catalogs those French poets whom she places in the tradition of literary and spiritual purity. Villon is the first and greatest because of his vision of affliction. Racine is included, but only because of *Phèdre* and the *Cantiques Spirituels*. Maurice Scève, Théophile de Viau, and Agrippa d'Aubigné are named as well. Being men of letters, the poets of the nineteenth century were gravely corrupted, but there are some vestiges of pure poetic genius, she says, in Lamartine, Vigny, Nerval, and Mallarmé. The rest of the romantic movement in French literature had already been roundly berated in an earlier passage of *L'Enracinement,* where Weil stated that Stendhal's *Le Rouge et le noir (The Red and the Black)* was an illustration of the French cult for Napoleon, a cult owing less to personal reverence for him than to the opportunities for advancement that his meritocracy afforded. "The Romantics," including Stendhal, she implies, "were children who felt bored because they no longer had before them the prospect of unrestricted social advancement. They sought literary glory as a substitute."[42] The contrast between the false greatness thus pursued by the romantics and the authentic purity of vision that represented truly great poetry to Weil is clearly drawn in a passage where she pays tribute to Saint Francis. "From the purely poetic point of view, without taking into account anything else, it is infinitely preferable to have written the Canticle of St. Francis of Assisi, that jewel of perfect beauty, than the entire works of Victor Hugo."[43]

In prose Weil cites Rabelais, Montaigne, Descartes, the Cardinal de Retz, Molière, Port-Royal,[44] Montesquieu, and Rousseau. She defines the genius of France represented in her Pantheon of pure artists as a Christian and Hellenic genius. Its spirit is also expressed in the architecture of Romanesque churches and in Gregorian chant. Earlier in *L'Enracinement* Weil speaks of the importance of founding a civilization on the principle of the spirituality of labor. "The thoughts relating to a presentiment of this vocation," she states, "and, which are scattered about in Rousseau, George Sand, Tolstoi, Proudhon, and Marx, in papal encyclicals, and elsewhere, are the only original thoughts of our time, the only ones we haven't borrowed from the Greeks."[45]

Chapter Five
Ways to the Divine: Knowledge

The pursuit of truth was the most powerful motivation in Simone Weil's short life. Her great devotion to Christ was first and foremost a commitment to him as the truth. Although rigid standards of intellectual probity were of great importance, knowledge was more than a strictly intellectual matter to her. It included manual skills, aesthetic sensibility, and a sense of community, as well as factual knowledge and wisdom. All these concerns are combined in the present chapter. If compartmentalizing Weil's holistic philosophy facilitates comprehension, one may say this chapter concentrates primarily on her philosophy of science and her philosophy of education.

Philosophy of Science

Often when the subject of science comes up in Weil's writings, the language in which her thoughts are expressed would almost make it seem as though she understood science to be an occult art, a mystique. "Scientific investigation is simply a form of religious contemplation."[1] Indeed, in the course of charting the development of science from ancient Greece to the twentieth century, she compares it with magic and alchemy as various approaches to the same human problems. Yet such an understanding of science would be a misrepresentation of Weil's philosophy.

Simone Weil's philosophy of science, like her thought in every domain, must not be considered in isolation. For she saw science as wholly integrated—with theology and art—into the fundamental aspiration of man, his search for truth, for meaning, for God. Science is the study of force and gravity; humanism is the study of grace and freedom. For centuries man had sensed a contradiction between the two without truly confronting it. Weil wished to find a way to integrate them in a holistic vision of truth. The right use of scientific inquiry is to contemplate the divinely conceived order of the world, as did the Greeks, so as to adore God as the perpetual geometer. Thus, science is not, according to Weil, an autonomous occult art that would take over the function of religion in man. Rather it is one of a number of coequal means that are subservient to man's principle end. It is, again, one of man's "ways to God."

It would be difficult to understand modern experimental science in this light without reference to a radically different model. For this reason it is important to realize that Weil makes distinctions among several different models of science, viewed in historical and methodological perspective. First she distinguishes the two most commonly acknowledged modern paradigms of science: classical science, based on Newtonian mechanics, and twentieth-century science, predicated on quantum physics. A third paradigm is that of Greek science, and often there is a fourth implicit in her writings, an ideal model not unlike that of the Greeks but taking into account certain insights attained by the moderns.

Classical Science

By classical science Weil means the conception of science generally adhered to from about the sixteenth century until 1900. Newton's mechanics provided the model for representing and analyzing natural phenomena, and the fundamental notion was that of work. Energy, a function of distance and force, was the common measure of all work. The aspect of classical science that pleased Weil most was its clear conception of necessity. "It is a necessity connected with time itself and it consists in the fact that time has a direction, so that it is never in any circumstances a matter of indifference in which direction a transformation takes place."[2] Sometimes referred to as entropy, this nonreversibility of a phenomenon of energy transformation was exploited richly by classical science in fields such as thermodynamics. Eventually, its adherents came to believe that "it would be possible, by calculation, measurement, and numerical equivalence, to read throughout all phenomena occurring in the universe simple variations of energy and entropy, conforming to a simple law."[3] A pernicious by-product of such aspirations was the notion of progress that hardened into the philosophy of logical positivism.

Weil sees a significant value in classical science. When it is properly practiced, she observes, it amounts to a means of purification in that "it tries to read behind all appearances that inexorable necessity which makes the world a place in which we do not count."[4] However, it gives a limited representation of reality. It presents us with a "slave's universe," since it interprets phenomena fundamentally in terms of manual labor. The significance of the basic lesson to be learned in classical science should not be taken lightly. One sees how Weil's idea of rightly using the principles of classical science conforms with her vision of truth as a whole: according to one of her former students, Weil taught that the law of entropy, and the whole science of energy in general, is predicated on a scientific restatement of Genesis 3:19, "By the sweat of your face you shall eat bread."[5]

Contemporary Science

The watershed event for modern science was the quantum theory advanced about 1900 by Max Planck. Planck held that radiant energy could be divided into finite quantities or parcels (quanta) in analyzing transformations of energy on an atomic or molecular scale. This theory made classical science obsolete by marking the return of discontinuity. Along with the discontinuous, another factor in the advent of a new science was the revolutionary precision of measurement. "Discontinuity, number, and smallness are enough to give rise to the atom, and the atom has returned to us, accompanied as always by chance and probability."[6] Classical science could not explain satisfactorily the motion of atoms as if they were very minute particles governed by the necessities of classical Newtonian mechanics. According to Weil, Planck's quantum theory, and the whole new scientific age it ushered in, is a step backward, rather than an advance. "Twentieth-century science is classical science with something taken away. Something taken, not something added, and least of all any relation to the good, for the lack of which classical science was a desert. What has been taken away is the analogy between the laws of nature and the conditions of work, that is to say, its very principle; and it is the quantum hypothesis that has removed it."[7]

Weil spent a great deal of time and effort in her last years studying and meditating upon the quantum theory. Deeply disturbed by the direction in which she saw it leading contemporary science, she concluded that its ultimate effect was to rob science of any meaning.

In the passage below she traces the circular reasoning of Max Planck's theory.

Planck's formula, composed of a constant whose source one cannot imagine and a number which corresponds to a probability, has no relation to any thought. How then is it justified? Its legitimacy is based on the number of calculations, and of experiments based upon these calculations, and of technical applications based upon the experiments, that have succeeded thanks to the formula. Planck himself claims no more than this. Once such a state of affairs is admitted, physics becomes a collection of signs and numbers combined in formulae, which are controlled by their applications. . . . The relation which is the principle of this science is simply the relation between algebraic formulae void of meaning, on the one hand, and technology on the other.[8]

One of the key problems of contemporary science, according to Weil, has been the notion of necessity versus probability in explaining the movement of atoms. It was noted above that the motion of atoms could not be explained as if they were minute particles governed by the necessities of classical mechanics. Because of the radical shift in size to the molecular scale, chance and probability replace necessity, without, however, any hiatus of causality. Here it is important to remember that chance is not incompatible with necessity. "Divorced from necessity, probability is no more than a résumé of statistics."[9] Planck's great error, according to Weil, was that he failed to arrive at a calculation of probabilities based not on numbers but on generalized number. "This is the crucial point for any critical examination of the quantum theory. . . . Planck was able to write a whole book . . . about the relation between contemporary science and philosophy, without making even the most distant allusion to it."[10]

It is not difficult to perceive that Weil did not consider classical science an ideal method of scientific inquiry. Yet she recognized its worth as a means of "purification," and she also was aware that the common-sense element in it preserved an important link with the rest of human thought. That link, she believed, was severed after 1900. For her, the method of studying atoms in contemporary science constitutes more than a change in scale (from that of normal human perception to the atomic scale). It is a change of kind. For example, contemporary physics translates heat into movement, once it enters the purely theoretical world of atoms. Thus left with movement alone, contemporary physics is unable properly to define entropy, since it is a notion that is essentially alien to movement. The most pernicious aspect of contemporary science that Weil analyzes is what she calls its lack of truth orientation. "All thought is an effort of interpretation of experience," she writes, and "all human effort is oriented."[11] Any field of inquiry must, in other words, be guided by a human value, and for science that value is some image (more or less defective as it may be) of truth.

Classical scientists had a representation of scientific truth which was certainly very defective, but they had one; whereas present-day scientists have nothing in their minds, however vague, remote, arbitrary, or improbable, which they can turn towards and call it truth. . . . So soon as truth disappears, utility takes its place. . . . Thus utility becomes something which the intelligence is no longer entitled to define or to judge, but only to serve.[12]

Two of Weil's criticisms of twentieth-century science would appear to apply to classical science as well, namely the concept of the negligible and its implications for the mathematical interpretation of geometrical figures. The great advances in the technology of measurement in the past century or two have fueled a comparable development in the experimental method of the natural sciences. However, both precision in measurement and the experimental method rest philosophically on the concept of the negligible. And no matter how great man's progress in these fields, the negligible can only be minimized, never eliminated. Philosophically, then, it is just as significant when minimized as it ever was.

What is neglected is always as large as the world, exactly as large, because the physicist neglects the whole difference between something that happens in front of his eyes and a perfectly closed, perfectly definite system which he conceives in his mind and represents on paper by symbols and signs; and this difference is the world itself. . . . The world is neglected because it has to be; and, since mathematics cannot be applied to phenomena at a lesser price, it is applied at the price of an infinite error.[13]

Of necessity, a scientific experiment creates an artificial world from which are carefully excluded all factors that would complicate the perfectly closed, perfectly defined situation created in the scientist's mind. Similarly, what is normally called a straight line drawn on a blackboard is infinitely different from one. But since it allows us to imagine one, it is not unrelated to one. "In a sense, an observation or an experiment are for a physicist exactly what a figure is for a geometer. . . . To the full extent that the notion of necessity plays a role in physics, physics is essentially the application of mathematics to nature at the price of an infinite error."[14]

Science in Ancient Greece

The man on the street in the 1980s, doubtless, would give very little credit to the ancient Greeks for the advancement of scientific knowledge. But for Simone Weil, Greek science was the beginning of classical science and contained all of it in germ. Eudoxus, she points out, invented integral calculus; Clausius discovered the law of entropy; and such seemingly revolutionary, "modern" concepts as the atom and the discontinuous were already carefully and brilliantly dealt with by the Greeks. There are several fundamental differences of perspective or of method between Greek science and classical or contemporary science, all of which demonstrate in Weil's view the superiority of the former. She believed the Greeks gave a richer and fuller representation of reality.

The most salient distinguishing characteristic of Greek science is the extraordinary importance it attributes to geometry. This is one of the lessons Weil learned best from the Greeks. Throughout her work she uses geometry to illustrate all kinds of principles—sociological, ethical, spiritual, physical. "The majority of them {students today} will always remain ignorant of the fact that nearly all our actions, the simple ones as well as the judiciously combined ones, are applications of geometrical relations, and that it is to geometrical necessity that we are in fact bound, as creatures enclosed in space and time."[15] Weil was fond of quoting Plato's aphorism that "God is ever a geometer," and the motto that graced the doorway of her philosophy class read: "None enters here unless he is a geometer."

The profound spirituality of Greek science is accounted for in great measure by the prominence it grants to geometry. For the spiritual purity of geometrical ideas is an image of the spiritual apprenticeship that is a precondition to becoming a geometer.

We are aware, each time we think of them, that the pure straight line, the pure angle, the pure triangle, are the work of an effort of attention in detaching itself from sensible phenomena and acts. . . . In order to think mathematically, we put aside the world; and at the end of this effort of renunciation the world is given us like a bonus. It is given, indeed, at the price of an infinite error, but nevertheless really given. By this renunciation of natural objects and by this contact with reality which goes with it as a gratuitous recompense, geometry is an image of virtue. To pursue the good also we have to turn away from material objects, and we receive the world in recompense; just as the line drawn in chalk is what we do while thinking of a straight line, so the virtuous act is what we do while loving God; and, like the chalk line, it contains an infinite error.[16]

Weil believed that geometry for the Greeks was analogous to ethics because it was a divine science, closely allied with religion. In fact, she often stated that it had arisen out of ancient Greek mystical traditions. She points out more than once that one of the meanings of *logos* is ratio, that there is an intimate relation between Christ, the *logos*, and the Greek geometrical notion of proportion that is near the heart of the order and meaning of creation.

The concept of equilibrium is also fundamental in Greek thought and is directly related to geometry. Archimedes' theory of the equilibrium of floating bodies, according to Weil, contains in germ the entire science of physics. The distance in water that a loaded ship sinks is seen today as the effect of a simple force, whereas Archimedes saw the ship's water line as a ratio between its own density and that of the water. In the modern version, says Weil, the poetic beauty and much of the precision are lost. Anaximander saw all of nature as a succession of mutually compensating disequilibriums. "It is from this that things arise and to it their destruction returns them, according to necessity; for things undergo from one another a punishment and an expiation because of their injustices according to the order of time."[17]

In the sense that classical science relates fundamentally to technology, so Greek science relates to art. It is a significant difference of orientation. "Classical science is without beauty; it neither touches the heart nor contains any wisdom," whereas for the Greeks "love, art, and science were scarcely separate aspects of the same movement of the soul towards the good."[18] The importance of proportions and geometrical ratios, as opposed to mathematical computations of numerical results, is reflected in a second contrast that Weil makes between classical and Greek science: "Instead of the relation between desire and the conditions of its accomplishment, the subject of Greek science is the relation between order and the conditions of order."[19] A final difference concerns the aim and orientation of Greek science. The all-important concept of blind necessity is regarded by moderns as an obstacle to be overcome, whereas the Greeks saw it as a basic aspect of divine order and hence a thing to be loved. "Both Greek science and classical science are concerned with the same conditions, but the aim of Greek science is totally different, it is the desire to contemplate in sensible phenomena an image of the good."[20]

Toward a New Science

It is rather ironic that Simone Weil ever used the term "new science," for the idea of progress in science was particularly repugnant to her. The ideal model of science that is implicit in many of her writings—and most explicit in "Foundation of a New Science"[21]—resembles Greek science far more than classical or contemporary science. In *L'Enracinement,* she suggests that the true definition of science is "the study of the beauty of the world."[22] A broader definition, suggested by her various writings on the subject, might look approximately like the following: the philosophy of the phenomena of the universe, understood as manifestations of the sovereign will of the creator. The purpose of such an inquiry is the same as that outlined by Weil in a letter to her brother André on the subject of Greek mathematics. "Purity of soul was their one concern; to 'imitate God' was the secret of it; the imitation of God was assisted by the study of mathematics, in so far as one conceived the universe to be subject to mathematical laws, which made the geometer an imitator of the supreme law giver."[23]

Weil's ideal model of science, then, would be built on the attempt to conceive the universe in relation to the good, a contemplation of God's order of the world, one of the ways to the divine. "Deliverance consists in reading limit and relation [in the sense of contingency] in all sensible phenomena without exception, with the same clarity and immediacy as a meaning in a printed text. The significance of a true science is to constitute a preparation for deliverance."[24] The modern scientist's aspiration toward total, value-free objectivity in his research would be rejected outright in Weil's scheme of things in order to restore the fundamental truth orientation that guided scientific inquiry for the Greeks. Her vision of a true science would be less susceptible to the danger of being used for the wrong aims.

Although this ideal science would resemble the Greek more than the contemporary model, it is properly called "new" in that it both incorporates insights from modern science and suggests directions that have yet to be explored. For example, she writes that the relatively recent mathematical concepts of group and invariant, along with the idea of set, should be applied in analyzing the fixed ratios and cyclical transformations of phenomena described by Anaximander as successive, mutually compensating ruptures of equilibrium. Among the potential new frontiers of future science, she postulates the study of a third principle of energy transformation. Classical science and contemporary science have confined their analysis almost exclusively to the conservation and the degradation of energy. "Up to now, science has not formulated a third principle but clearly it is needed, to balance the degradation of energy; for otherwise maximum entropy would already have been reached everywhere, and everything would be motionless and dead. The transformation of inorganic into organic matter, however, is the opposite of a degradation, and this transformation is occurring continually."[25] Such directions as the one suggested above are so clearly related to philosophical questions of value that Weil's insistence on a new science built upon a fundamental truth orientation becomes even more crucial. If scientists are to explore the very mystery of creation, they must be guided in everything by a vision of truth and of the good. They must consciously embrace their fields of scientific inquiry as mutually related and mutually illuminating ways to God.

Philosophy of Education

Simone Weil was trained as a teacher of philosophy. Even though she actually had less than five years' experience as a classroom teacher in French lycées, education was of supreme importance to her. Aside from her formal classroom work, she found herself seeking out every opportunity to instruct young people and to infect them with the intense thirst for truth that possessed her. While working in the grape harvests of the Ardèche she gave arithmetic lessons to a village urchin, and during her final working days in London she took it upon herself to tutor the children of her landlady. Her involvement in free workers' universities likewise revealed the strategic importance of education in her vision of a just society.

Her pedagogical methods were a reflection of her personal values and of the influences of her masters. Embracing Marx's goal of preparing the way for a society "in which the degrading division of work into manual work and intellectual work will be abolished," she taught that there have been two basic social classes throughout history: those who have power to manipulate things (the workers) and those who manipulate words (intellectuals and priests). Recalling Alain's assertion that words are the tools for manipulating men, she proclaimed that workers must gain power over words. In Weil's view, the proletarian revolution could be accomplished if exploited workers could simply take possession of culture. That act in itself would constitute the revolution.

Reports of headmistresses and inspectors from the Ministry of Education were mixed regarding Weil's effectiveness as a teacher. They considered her intellectual gifts to be impressive but often found her lessons too difficult for the students, and they criticized her delivery: speaking in a monotone voice without looking at her pupils. Above all, however, she was accused of tendentious teaching, too heavily emphasizing her own personal philosophy. For the most part, her students' performances on the *baccalauréat* confirmed the negative reports. Except for the class at Bourges, relatively few were able to pass after their year of study with Weil. Of course, she was supremely uninterested in teaching with a view to high scores on a competitive examination whose value she considered minimal. Her passionately held opinions and fierce love of justice very naturally inspired the young women in her charge, however, as is clearly seen in a letter from one of her students at Le Puy, written two years after her tenure there. She said they had all been deeply influenced by their teacher, indeed "radicalized"; Weil had led them to become "malcontents" in the face of injustice and oppression.[26]

There are two of Weil's pedagogical doctrines that reveal perhaps most clearly the kind of teacher she was. First, as texts for studying philosophy she preferred increasingly to use those writings of the highest literary quality, whether or not they were overtly concerned with philosophical topics. Second, she assigned a great many written compositions, since she believed the act of writing was an indispensable tool for disciplining one's thinking processes.

It is also significant that Weil's vision of a just and humane French society in *L'Enracinement* greatly stresses the role of education. The great texts of philosophy and literature need to be translated into the language of factory workers and peasants. For the former, the teaching of science should be focused on the principles of mechanical energy that govern the fruitfulness of their labor. For the latter (the peasants), it should revolve around the solar energy cycle, thus suffusing agricultural labor with the kind of poetry found in Christ's parables of the fields. Indeed, in a larger sense, Weil's philosophy of education envisioned the clear and intimate connectedness of all vocations to the life of Christ in such a way as to foster a brotherhood of productive sacrifice. Her unusual way of bringing together the study of physical science, philosophy, folklore, religion, and literature was an ingenious attempt ,to make the world of work into a living organism, a community devoted to high ideals and inspired by its clear relation to the deepest aspirations of the collective soul. Rootedness in such a vision of human society would give each person in every station of life an assurance of his worth and purpose in the grand design.

Mystique of Study

One of the most intriguing essays in Simone Weil's work is the one in *Attente de Dieu* entitled "Réflexions sur le bon usage des études scolaires en vue de l'amour de Dieu" (Reflections on the right use of school studies with a view to the love of God). It contains some of her most important thinking on the nature of education. As her reflections on (and experiences of) the conditions of working-class people led her to a mystique of labor, so her vision of what it means really to learn entails a kind of mystique of study.

Evoking in her title Pascal's equally intriguing "Prière pour demander à Dieu le bon usage des maladies" (Prayer to ask of God the proper use of sickness), she places school studies squarely in the context of the all-encompassing quest for truth. Rather than perpetuating the sterile modern skepticism that values the quest itself—whether or not answers are found—she argues that a genuine pursuit of true answers is absolutely indispensable. Yet she adds that even if one is not gifted or interested in a given discipline, the effort of real attention expended on a problem of geometry, for example, is never lost, even if the solution is not found. The ultimate goal beyond the answer should be to enhance the attention that forms the very substance of prayer. It is important to study with the goal of performing an exercise correctly then, not with extrinsic goals such as grades and test scores. But one must have faith that God will reward the *attente* ("attention," "attentiveness," "waiting") in the experience of prayer, an extrinsic goal of a very different order.

One must contemplate carefully each error and each correction, with full consciousness of one's mediocrity. "It is perhaps even more useful to contemplate our stupidity than our sin."[27] It is in this sense that properly expended efforts in study are never wasted, even when one fails to find the correct answer. Such efforts of attention, however, are not to be confused with muscular effort. Attention does not depend on will, but on desire, the joy of learning, just as in spiritual life there must be a desire for God, rather than a strong willpower. Attention is a negative effort, the ability to leave one's thought empty, suspended, available (one thinks of Gide's *disponibilité*), penetrable by truth. All errors, according to Weil, result from the inclination to jump to conclusions, rather than remaining patiently open to the arrival of truth. "The cause is always that we have wanted to be too active; we have wanted to carry out a search. . . . We do not obtain the most precious gifts by going in search of them but by waiting for them."[28]

For Simone Weil, then, academic study is at bottom like a sacrament. Just as the Spirit of Truth cannot be sought out by man, so the student must not pursue truth too aggressively. One must wait patiently, attentively, expectantly, until one is found by truth. "In every school exercise there is a special way of waiting upon truth, setting our hearts upon it, yet not allowing ourselves to go out in search of it."[29] The parable Weil uses to illustrate the meaning of study is the one of the wise virgins with lamps and oil waiting for the husband who will serve them at the marriage feast. The slave who works and exerts himself in service is not appreciated; it is the one who simply waits whom the master will in fact reward.

The thread that runs unbroken through Weil's meandering meditations on knowledge—whether philosophy of science or philosophy of education—is the quest for truth. In all the varied preoccupations of her life and thought, it may be said that she remained ever a student. The rigorous intellectual discipline instilled in her during her years in French schools was never to be outgrown. So thoroughly trained was she in *explication de texte* that she viewed all of reality as a text to be explicated, or "read" (in the special sense in which she used the notion of *lecture*). But the act of reading was much more than an academic exercise. It was to involve not only the brain but also the heart and even the body. This "total" concept of knowledge—a contemplation of the beauty of the world with all one's heart, soul, body, and mind—reveals the perspective from which Weil was able to understand knowledge (as she had understood beauty) as one of the most promising "ways to the divine."

Chapter Six
Conclusion

Simone Weil died in near-total obscurity in a foreign land. Her published works during her lifetime consisted only of a number of articles. Yet the message of which she believed herself to be an unworthy vessel was destined to reach more and more lives across the years. Thanks to Gustave Thibon's efforts, the Plon publishers released *La Pesanteur et la grâce* in 1947. In 1949 Albert Camus, who was directing the "Espoir" collection[1] for Gallimard, brought out *L'Enracinement,* and Father Perrin published *Attente de Dieu* through La Colombe the following year.

Up to the publication of *La Pesanteur et la grâce* in 1947, then, there was no significant awareness of Weil's work in the literary world. The articles that she had published during her lifetime had always appeared in journals of rather narrow circulation, such as *La Révolution prolétarienne, Les Cahiers du Sud,* and *Libres Propos.* Her public, if the term may be used here, consisted chiefly of readers with ties to the revolutionary syndicalist movement, those with an interest in the extinct civilization of the Cathares, or followers of Alain.

The immense popularity and respect that Camus enjoyed in the 1950s were significant factors in the rapidly spreading interest in Weil in that decade, since he continued to publish several of her books in Gallimard's "Espoir" collection. He was convinced that hers was one of the most important voices to be heard in the crisis of postwar reconstruction of the French nation. His preface to *L'Enracinement* was certainly instrumental in calling attention to her work. He called her "le seul grand esprit de notre temps."[2] Articles by Albert Béguin,[3] Gabriel Marcel,[4] François Mauriac,[5] and Georges Bataille[6] hailed the insights of her first several books (1949–51). The first important book-length studies, by Marie-Magdeleine Davy[7] and Thibon and Perrin,[8] appeared in the early 1950s, and from that point on Weil's name has come to occupy a rather important place in French thought.

In England and the United States, the translations of Weil appeared shortly after the originals: *Waiting for God* in 1951, *Gravity and Grace* and *The Need for Roots* in 1952, and so on up to the present. Most of the critical attention accorded them came from the Catholic intelligentsia, who focused largely on her political and religious thought. Undoubtedly the most influential praise of Weil's work in the English-speaking world was T. S. Eliot's preface to *The Need for Roots,* in which he declared that she was a writer of a "genius akin to that of the saints."[9] Eliot's praise, of course, was hardly unqualified. He was aware of the patience a reader needs in order to sift through to the pure nuggets of wisdom in her writings. Indeed, the critics were far from forming a unanimous chorus of approbation. Graham Greene decried what he called spiritual pride and posings in her refusals of baptism, and he expressed little sympathy with the contradictions of her unorthodox theology in *Waiting for God.*[10] Kenneth Rexroth called *The Need for Roots* "a collection of egregious nonsense surpassed only by the deranged fantasies of the chauvinist Péguy."[11] Of her work in general he commented that "hers was a spastic, moribund, intellectual and spiritual agony. . . . Simone Weil assaulted the Garden of Gethsemane, and, as is so often the case, was broken on the gate."[12]

Perhaps more balanced evaluations of Weil's life and thought came in 1952 from Dwight MacDonald,[13] who was also responsible for the publication in *Politics* of Mary McCarthy's translation of "*L'Iliade,* ou le poème de la force," and from Alfred Kazin in the *New Yorker;*[14] in addition, E. W. F. Tomlin's fine little monograph appeared in 1954.[15] The majority of Weil's important writings were published in the 1950s. The milestones in Weil scholarship since then include the biography by Simone Pétrement,[16] the bibliography by Janet Patricia Little,[17] and Sir Richard Rees's *Simone Weil: A Sketch for a Portrait.*[18]

In 1960, on the occasion of Camus's tragic death, *Le Monde* published interviews of several of his friends, among whom was included Mme Selma Weil. She expressed the hope that the death of Camus, who had taken such an active role in publishing her daughter's works, would not curtail the work that remained to be completed. M. Robert Gaillardot, an engineer with a deep interest in Simone's writings, offered his help to Mme Weil. It was the beginning of a close working relationship, and through it there eventually was organized a research group (now connected to the

Association pour l'étude de la pensée de Simone Weil) that has worked on the Weil manuscripts, has published at least two collections of critical essays, and is currently preparing the publication of Weil's complete works. The most recent addition to Weil studies in this country is more evidence of the ongoing vitality of her writings and their capacity to excite the human mind and spirit across the years. George Abbott White's *Simone Weil: Interpretations of a Life*[19] is an excellent collection of essays that grew out of a seminar and public lecture series on Weil that he directed at Massachusetts Institute of Technology in 1975–76. And the recently organized American Weil Society now has an annual colloquy where students of Weil's work may share their insights. Even in a town with a population of 150,000 a symposium recently organized by a Roman Catholic parish was able to attract an audience of two hundred to hear scholars speak on the significance of Weil's life and thought.

It may be said that Simone Weil's following, although it will never be of the proportions of those of a Malraux or a Camus, is a deeply devoted one. There is even an almost cult-like fascination with her. A sort of French Dorothy Day, she left an example of uncompromising pursuit of an ideal that wears well through the years. No doubt, she would have taken little pleasure in having her own commemorative stamp or in having a Paris street named after her (a goal toward which the Weil Society in France has been working for some time). Yet these mundane matters have their own significance in reflecting the deep appeal that writers come to exert on their public. And are they not after all another means of preserving the rootedness, the *enracinement* that connects the present generation with the spiritual nourishment it may draw from the culture of the past?

It is rather speculative to talk about the influence of one writer on another but perhaps enlightening to take note of the kind of writers and thinkers who were interested in a given figure. In Weil's case one is struck by the caliber of those who have considered her important enough to write about. In addition to those cited in the last few pages, there are articles on Simone Weil by such writers as Martin Buber, Thomas Merton, Malcolm Muggeridge, Iris Murdoch, Herbert Read, and Susan Sontag. One of the pitfalls that have victimized Weil scholars is the tendency toward uncritical adulation, although there is also a vein of invective in such critics as Greene and Rexroth. Camus's and Eliot's encomiums were quoted above. Muggeridge called Weil "the most luminous intelligence of the twentieth century."[20] But in the face of the bitter denunciation as well as the wild praise one is reminded of Weil's repeated conviction that it was ultimately of no importance whether anyone thought of her as intelligent or creative. She refused to accept praise of her intellectual gifts and only asked that people honestly confront the question of whether what she said and wrote was truth. She herself did not count. It was that which she contained (she sometimes referred to it as a "mine of pure gold") and to which she sought to be a faithful witness that mattered.

Few writers have taken more seriously their role of prophetic witness, and few have taken up the mantle of prophetic authority with more humility than Simone Weil. In her pure desire to be used ("to be pushed by God toward my neighbor as a pencil is pushed by me across the paper")[21] she lived out admirably the doctrine of mediation that is so central to her entire philosophy. It is a sign of true wisdom that rather than seeking to take the kingdom of God by storm she saw and understood the immense power of patience, attention, nonaction. The most powerful bridges *(metaxu)* between God and man are also the humblest: *malheur,* obedience, waiting, beauty, ratio, necessity, labor.

All these ways to God that Weil discerned have to do with what is perhaps her most profound insight into the meaning of existence. It is what struck Vladimir Volkoff when he first encountered her writings: that Christian charity and Greek geometry spring from the same divine source; that truth has a shape, a form; that there is a secret formula, a mean proportional, built into the order of the universe. This, the most profound and effectual mediation, is the *logos,* Jesus the Christ, whose presence was forever engraved in Simone Weil at that moment in 1938 while she repeated the words of George Herbert's poem "Love," itself a *metaxu* culminating the pilgrim's wait for God.

Abbreviations

AD: *Attente de Dieu*

C: *Cahiers*

CO: *La Condition ouvrière*

CS: *La Connaissance surnaturelle*

EL: *Ecrits de Londres et dernières lettres*

ENR: *L'Enracinement*

GG: *Gravity and Grace*

IPF: *The Iliad, Poem of Force*

NFR: *The Need for Roots*

OAL: *Oppression and Liberty*

OEL: *Oppression et liberté*

OSN: *On Science, Necessity, and the Love of God*

PG: *La Pesanteur et la grâce*

PSO: *Pensées sans ordre concernant l'amour de Dieu*

SG: *La Source grecque*

SLS: *Sur la science*

SWL: *Simone Weil: A Life* (Pétrement)

SWR: *The Simone Weil Reader*

VSW: *La Vie de Simone Weil* (Pétrement)

WG: *Waiting for God*

Notes and References

Preface

1. "Il est donc nécessaire de faire un tri pour savoir ses pensées et aussi la vérité de ses pensées; c'est elle-même qui nous y invite." Joseph-Marie Perrin and Gustave Thibon, *Simone Weil telle que nous l'avons connue* (Paris, 1952), p. 111 (my tr.).

2. "A d'autres de discerner ce que cela vaut et d'où cela vient." *Pensées sans ordre concernant l'amour de Dieu* (Paris, 1962), p. 133 (my tr.); subsequently referred to as PSO. Contains miscellaneous essays, letters, and fragments concerning Weil's religious thought in her last three or four years.

Chapter One

1. "Cher tante Gabrielle, je t'envoie cette lettre, car tu seras trés étonnée, je ne t'et pas félicité pour la nouvelle année. Je t'en félicite mintenan. Qu'est-ce que tu pence de la situation (pour la gerre)?" Simone Pétrement, *La vie de Simone Weil, avec des lettres et d'autres textes inédits de Simone Weil*, 2 volumes (Paris, 1973), 1:33 (my tr.); subsequently referred to as VSW.

2. Tr. Raymond Rosenthal, *Simone Weil: A Life* (New York, 1976), p. 29; subsequently referred to as SWL. "Elle paraissait oublier à un rare degré tout intérêt ou désir personnel, ne se passionnant que pour de nobles causes et sans rancune, sans colère pour ce qui la touchait seule." VSW, 1:69–70.

3. Tr. Emma Craufurd, *Waiting for God* (New York, 1951), p. 64; subsequently referred to as WG. "Je ne regrettais pas les succès extérieurs, mais de ne pouvoir espérer aucun accès à ce royaume transcendant où les hommes authentiquement grands sont seuls à entrer et où habite la vérité. J'aimais mieux mourir que de vivre sans elle. Après des mois de ténèbres intérieures j'ai eu soudain et pour toujours la certitude que n'importe quel être humain, même si ses facultés naturelles sont presque nulles, pénètre dans ce royaume de la vérité réservé au génie, si seulement il désire la vérité et fait perpétuellement un effort d'attention pour l'atteindre." *Attente de Dieu* (Paris, 1966), pp. 38–39; subsequently referred to as AD. The passage cited comes from a long letter to Father Perrin, which he entitles "Autobiographie spirituelle." AD consists of six letters and five essays left to Perrin by Weil before her departure from Marseilles in 1942, all concerning her religious philosophy.

4. WG, 64. "La certitude que j'avais reçue, c'était que quand on désire du pain on ne reçoit pas des pierres." AD, 39.

5. SWL, 26. "Enfant déjà elle voulait avec résolution faire quelque chose de sa vie et craignait par-dessus tout de manquer sa mort." VSW, 1:65.

6. Jacques Cabaud, *Simone Weil: A Fellowship in Love* (New York, 1964), p. 37.

7. SWL, 25. "Simone lui doit peut-être l'approfondissement de sa révolte, le discernement des causes les plus vraies de la tyrannie, le refus des solutions fausses qui ramènent une tyrannie plus lourde. Il est certainement pour quelque chose dans la lucidité et la force de la pensée qu'elle a montrées plus tard dans le domaine politique. Sans lui, elle aurait peut-être gaspillé son dévouement au service de quelque parti. Mais dans sa volonté d'être toujours du côté de l'esclave, elle a rencontré son maître plutôt qu'elle n'a construit à partir de sa doctrine." VSW, 1:64.

8. Cabaud, *Simone Weil*, p. 32.

9. "Elle n'était pas laide, comme on l'a dit, mais prématurément voûtée et vieillie par l'ascétisme et la maladie, et seuls ses yeux admirables surgeaient dans ce naufrage de la beauté." Perrin and Thibon, *Simone Weil*, p. 128 (my tr.).

10. SWL, 28, "Du reste, son costume devint de plus en plus celui d'un pauvre ou d'un moine, qui s'habille aux moindres frais en y consacrant le moins de temps possible." VSW, 1:67.

11. Tr. James Kirkup, *Memoirs of a Dutiful Daughter* (New York: World Publishers, 1959), p. 252. "Je réussis un jour à l'approcher. Je ne sais plus comment la conversation s'engagea; elle déclara d'un ton trenchant qu'une seule chose comptait aujourd'hui sur terre: la révolution qui donnerait à manger à tout le monde. Je rétorquai de façon non moins péremptoire, que le problème n'était pas de faire le bonheur des hommes, mais de trouver un sens à leur existence. Elle me toisa: 'On voit bien que vous n'avez jamais eu faim,' dit-elle." Simone de Beauvoir, *Mémoires d'une jeune fille rangée* (Paris: Gallimard, 1958), p. 237.

12. SWL, 261. "Toutes les fois que je traverse une période de maux de tête, je me demande si le moment de mourir n'est pas venu. Plus d'une fois je me suis trouvée près de me résoudre à mourir, de crainte d'une déchéance pire que la mort; au point que, pour écarter le risque de succomber sous le coup d'une dépression irraisonnée, j'ai décidé de ne jamais prendre une telle résolution (sauf circonstances exceptionnelles) qu'à une échéance de six mois ou d'un an." VSW, 2:81.

13. SWL, 235–36. "Le moindre acte de bienveillance . . . exige qu'on triomphe de la fatigue, de l'obsession du salaire. . . . De même la pensée demande un effort presque miraculeux pour s'élever au-dessus des conditions dans lesquelles on vit." VSW, 2:35.

14. WG, 66–67. "Ce contact avec le malheur avait tué ma jeunesse. Jusque-là je n'avais pas eu l'expérience du malheur, sinon du mien propre, qui, étant le mien, me paraissait de peu d'importance, et qui d'ailleurs n'était qu'un demi-malheur, étant biologique et non social. Je savais bien qu'il y avait beaucoup de malheur dans le monde, j'en étais obsédée, mais je ne l'avais jamais constaté par un contact prolongé. Etant en usine . . . le malheur des autres est entré dans ma chair et dans mon âme. . . . J'ai reçu là pour toujours la marque de l'esclavage. . . . Depuis je me suis toujours regardée comme une esclave." AD, 41–42.

15. SWL, 216. "Quelque chose en elle avait été brisé, peut-être, et son caractère s'en était adouci. Elle n'était plus tout à fait 'la terrible,' comme l'appelait auparavant Cancouët." VSW, 1:432.

16. "Une oppression évidemment inexorable et invincible n'engendre pas comme réaction immédiate la révolte, mais la soumission." *La Condition ouvrière* (Paris, 1951), p. 145 (my tr.); subsequently referred to as CO. In addition to the journal she kept during her year in the factories (1934–35), this book contains twenty-four letters and six articles written between 1934 and 1942 on the working-class condition.

17. Cabaud, *Simone Weil*, p. 128.

18. WG, 67. "Là, j'ai eu soudain la certitude que le christianisme est par excellence la religion des esclaves, que les esclaves ne peuvent pas ne pas y adhérer, et moi parmi les autres." AD, 43.

19. WG, 67–68. "Quelque chose de plus fort que moi m'a obligée, pour la première fois de ma vie, à me mettre à genoux." AD, 43.

20. WG, 68–69. "Je croyais le réciter seulement comme un beau poème, mais à mon insu cette récitation avait la vertu d'une prière. C'est au cours d'une de ces récitations que . . . le Christ lui-même est descendu et m'a prise." AD, 44–45.

21. Cabaud, *Simone Weil*, p. 182.

22. "La non-violence n'est bonne que si elle est efficace." *Cahiers*, 3 volumes (Paris, 1951), 1:153 (my tr.); subsequently referred to as C.

23. "Parce qu'il ne peut pas arrêter cette guerre, et que, si elle a lieu, il ne peut pas ne pas y prendre part." C, 153.

24. Cabaud, *Simone Weil*, p. 194.

25. "La peine et le péril sont indispensables à cause de ma conformation mentale. . . . Le malheur répandu sur la surface du globe terrestre m'obsède et m'accable au point d'annuler mes facultés, et je ne puis les récupérer et me délivrer de cette obsession que si j'ai moi-même une large part de danger et de souffrance." *Ecrits de Londres et dernières lettres* (Paris, 1957), p. 199 (my tr.); subsequently referred to as EL.

26. Cabaud, *Simone Weil*, p. 294.

27. "Les intelligences entièrement, exclusivement abandonnées et vouées à la vérité ne sont utilisables pour aucun être humain, y compris

celui dans lequel elles résident. Je n'ai pas la possibilité d'utiliser ma
propre intelligence; comment pourrais-je la mettre à la disposition de
Philip? C'est elle qui m'utilise, et elle-même obéit sans réserves—J'espère
du moins qu'il en est ainsi—à ce qui lui paraît être la lumière de la vérité."
VSW, 507 (my tr.).
    28. "Père, au nom du Christ, accorde-moi ceci. Que je sois hors
d'état de faire correspondre à aucune de mes volontés aucun mouvement
du corps, aucune ébauche même de mouvement, comme un paralytique
complet. Que je sois hors d'état d'enchaîner par la moindre liaison deux
pensées, même les plus simples, comme un de ces idiots complets qui non
seulement ne savent ni compter ni lire, mais n'ont même jamais pu apprendre à parler. Que je sois insensible à toute espèce de douleur et de
joie, et incapable d'aucun amour pour aucun être, pour aucune chose, ni
même pour moi-même, comme les vieillards complètement gâteux. . . .
Que tout cela [body, senses, intelligence, sensibility, love] soit arraché à
moi, dévoré par Dieu, transformé en substance du Christ, et donné à
manger à des malheureux dont le corps et l'âme manquent de toutes les
espèces de nourriture. Et que moi, je sois un paralysé, aveugle, sourd,
idiot, et gâteux." La Connaissance surnaturelle (Paris, 1950), pp. 204–5
(my tr.); subsequently referred to as CS. This book is composed of the
last notebooks, beginning with the time of Weil's departure from Marseilles in 1942 and continuing into the last days of her life.

Chapter Two

    1. SWL, 27. "Beaucoup de ses anciens camarades furent surpris
plus tard de la trouver si humaine, quand ils purent lire ses écrits. Moi-
même, je fus étonnée par certains traits de sensibilité qu'ils révèlent."
VSW, 66.
    2. Simone Weil (ed. Georges Hourdin), La Pesanteur et la grâce
(Paris, 1948), p. 183; subsequently referred to as PG.
    3. Tr. Arthur Wills, Gravity and Grace (New York, 1952), p. 200;
subsequently referred to as GG. "Ce monde est la porte d'entrée. C'est
une barrière. Et, en même temps, c'est le passage." PG, 146. The first
book by Weil to reach the public, PG was a selection of her most striking
meditations chosen from her notebooks and presented by Gustave Thibon.
    4. GG, 200. "Toute séparation est un lien." PG, 146.
    5. GG, 188. "Chaque être crie en silence pour être lu autrement."
PG, 135.
    6. GG, 156. "Méthode d'investigation: dès qu'on a pensé quelque
chose, chercher en quel sens le contraire est vrai." PG, 107.
    7. GG, 168. "La religion en tant que source de consolation est un
obstacle à la véritable foi: en ce sens l'athéisme est une purification." PG,
117.

8. "Nous n'avons pas à baptiser, morte, celle qui n'a pas voulu être baptisée vivante." Perrin and Thibon, *Simone Weil*, p. 173 (my tr.).

9. "Il y a entre Simone Weil et un philosophe purement spéculatif, la même différence qu'entre un guide et un géographe. Le géographe étudie objectivement une région: il en décrit les structures, en évalue les richesses, etc. Le guide, lui, conduit, par le chemin le plus court, à un but donné. De son point de vue, tout ce qui rapproche de ce but est bon, tout ce qui en éloigne est mauvais. Or Simone Weil est avant tout un guide sur le chemin entre l'âme et Dieu, et beaucoup de ses formules gagnent à être interprétées, non pas comme une description du pays traversé, mais comme des conseils aux voyageurs." Perrin and Thibon, *Simone Weil*, p. 170 (my tr.).

10. Tr. Richard Rees, *On Science, Necessity, and the Love of God* (London, 1968), p. 12; subsequently referred to as OSN. "Un mystique authentique . . . le père de la mystique occidentale." *La Source grecque* (Paris, 1953), p. 80; subsequently referred to as SG. "Dieu dans Platon" was written in Marseilles and New York between 1940 and 1942. It is rather elliptical in style, since it was taken from her notebooks of the period. In addition to "Dieu dans Platon" and her essay on the *Iliad*, SG's contents include translations and fragmentary commentaries—most of which were written between 1939 and 1943 in her notebooks—on Heraclitus, Sophocles, and other ancient Greek writers.

11. OSN, 99. "La sagesse de Platon n'est pas une philosophie, une recherche de Dieu par les moyens de la raison humaine. Une telle recherche, Aristote l'a faite aussi bien qu'on peut la faire. Mais la sagesse de Platon n'est pas autre chose qu'une orientation de l'âme vers la grâce." SG, 89.

12. OSN, 108. "L'être qui est vraiment être, le monde intelligible, est *produit* par le Bien suprême, il en émane. Le monde matériel est *fabriqué*." SG, 101, italics hers.

13. OSN, 110. "Le captif dont les chaînes sont tombées traverse la caverne. Il ne discerne rien; d'ailleurs il est vraiment dans la pénombre. Il ne lui servirait à rien de s'arrêter et d'examiner ce qui l'entoure. Il faut qu'il marche, quoique ce soit au prix de mille douleurs et sans savoir où il va. La volonté ici est seule en cause." SG, 103.

14. OSN, 110–11. "Il n'y a plus à faire des efforts de volonté, il faut seulement se maintenir en état d'attente et regarder ce dont l'éclat est à peu près insupportable." SG, 103.

15. "L'immobilité attentive et fidèle qui dure indéfiniment et que ne peut ébranler aucun choc." AD, 193 (my tr.).

16. OSN, 124. "La contemplation de la beauté implique le détachement. Une chose perçue comme belle est une chose à quoi on ne touche pas, à quoi on ne veut pas toucher, de peur d'y nuire. Pour transmuer en

énergie spirituellement utilisable l'énergie fournie par les autres objets de désir, il faut un acte de détachement, de refus." SG, 120.

17. OSN, 113. "Pour le passage des ténèbres à la contemplation du soleil, il faut des intermédiaires, des *metaxu.*" SG, 106.

18. OSN, 113. "Car partout où il y a apparence de contradiction, il y a corrélation des contraires, c'est-à-dire rapport. Toutes les fois qu'une contradiction s'impose à l'intelligence, elle est contrainte de concevoir un rapport qui transforme la contradiction en corrélation et par suite l'âme est tirée vers le haut." SG, 106.

19. OSN, 117. "L'un dans Platon est Dieu, l'indéfini est la matière. Dès lors la parole: '*le nombre constitue la médiation entre l'un et l'indéfini*' a de singulières résonances." SG, 111.

20. OSN, 129. "Ce beau absolu, divin, dont la contemplation rend ami de Dieu, c'est Dieu sous l'attribut de la beauté. Ce n'est pas encore l'aboutissement; cela correspond donc à l'être dans la *République* (le Verbe)." SG, 126.

21. GG, 45, 48, italics are translator's. "Tous les mouvements naturels de l'âme sont régis par des lois analogues à celles de la pesanteur matérielle. La grâce seule fait exception. . . . Descendre d'un mouvement où la pesanteur n'a aucune part. . . . La pesanteur fait descendre, l'aile fait monter: quelle aile à la deuxième puissance peut faire descendre sans pesanteur? . . . S'abaisser, c'est monter à l'égard de la pesanteur morale. La pesanteur morale nous fait tomber vers le haut." PG, 11, 13.

22. OSN, 118. "Impossible de dire plus clairement que l'aile est *un organe surnaturel,* qu'elle est la grâce." SG, 113, italics hers.

23. Cf. Robert S. Cohen, "Parallels and the Possibility of Influence between Simone Weil's *Waiting for God* and Samuel Beckett's *Waiting for Godot,*" *Modern Drama* 6 (February 1964):425–36.

24. WG, 145. "Dieu et toutes les créatures, cela est moins que Dieu seul." AD, 131.

25. WG, 145. "Dieu s'est par l'acte créateur nié lui-même, comme le Christ nous a prescrit de nous nier nous-mêmes." AD, 131.

26. WG, 89. "Si on tombe en persévérant dans l'amour jusqu'au point où l'âme ne peut plus retenir le cri 'Mon Dieu, pourquoi m'as-tu abandonné,' si on demeure en ce point sans cesser d'aimer, on finit par toucher quelque chose qui n'est plus le malheur, qui n'est pas la joie, qui est l'essence centrale, essentielle, pure, non sensible, commune à la joie et à la souffrance, et qui est l'amour même de Dieu." AD, 69.

27. WG, 135. "Celui dont l'âme rest orientée vers Dieu pendant qu'elle est percée d'un clou se trouve cloué sur le centre même de l'univers." AD, 120.

28. "Dieu est une sphère infinie dont le centre est partout et la circonférence nulle part." Quoted in CS, 23 (my tr.). Hermes Trisme-

gistus—not to be confused with Hermes, messenger of the gods in Greek mythology—was the Greek name for the Egyptian deity "Thoth the very great," reputed author of gnostic treatises known as the *Hermetica*.

29. WG, 97–98. "Un tel amour n'aime pas les êtres et les choses en Dieu, mais de chez Dieu. Etant auprès de Dieu il abaisse de là son regard, confondu avec le regard de Dieu, sur tous les êtres et sur toutes les choses. Il faut être catholique, c'est-à-dire n'être relié par aucun fil à rien qui soit créé, sinon la totalité de la création." AD, 79.

30. WG, 121. ". . . sensation de culpabilité et de souillure, que le crime devrait logiquement produire et ne produit pas. Le mal habite dans l'âme du criminel sans y être senti. Il est senti dans l'âme de l'innocent malheureux. Tout se passe comme si l'état de l'âme qui par essence convient au criminel avait été séparé du crime et attaché au malheur; et même à proportion de l'innocence des malheureux." AD, 103.

31. "Il désigne pour elle la transcendance, mais un transcendance au-delà des religions qui l'interprètent." Marie-Magdeleine Davy, *Introduction au message de Simone Weil* (Paris, 1954), p. iii (my tr.).

32. "La masse immense et malheureuse des incroyants." AD, 19 (my tr.).

33. Thomas Altizer, *The Gospel of Christian Atheism* (Philadelphia: The Westminster Press, 1966).

34. WG, 175. "Il n'y a pas dans la vie humaine de région qui soit le domaine de la nature. Le surnaturel est présent partout en secret, sous mille formes diverses la grâce et le péché mortel sont partout." AD, 167.

35. *Anathema sit* (literally, "Let him be accursed") is the ecclesiastical formula pronounced in excommunication.

36. WG, 53. "J'ai peur de ce patriotisme de l'Eglise qui existe dans certains milieux catholiques." AD, 24.

37. " 'Tu ne me chercherais pas si tu ne m'avais trouvé.' . . . L'homme n'a pas à chercher, ni même à croire en Dieu. Il doit seulement refuser son amour à tout ce qui est autre que Dieu." PSO, 42 (my tr.).

38. WG, 185. "Chaque religion est une combinaison originale de vérités explicites et de vérités implicites; ce qui est explicite chez l'une est implicite dans telle autre." AD, 179.

39. Weil "croyait au sujet de l'Eucharistie la même chose que moi." Raymond-Léopold Bruckberger, "Trois Témoignages sur Simone Weil— I," *Cahiers Simone Weil* 2, no. 4 (December 1979):181 (my tr.).

40. Cf. the fiction of a Julien Green, for example, where houses or rooms take on an almost human existence through the suffering endured "entre ces murs." More than a variation on the romantic's pathetic fallacy, this phenomenon is an illustration of Weil's "transfer" concept.

41. GG, 172. "Une inspiration divine opère infailliblement, irrésistiblement, si on n'en détourne pas l'attention, si on ne la refuse pas. Il

n'y a pas un choix à faire en sa faveur, il suffit de ne pas refuser de reconnaître qu'elle est." PG, 121.

42. "Je crois en Dieu, à la Trinité, à l'Incarnation, à la Rédemption, à l'Eucharistie, aux ensiegnements de l'Evangile." PSO, 149 (my tr.).

43. "J'adhère par l'amour à la vérité parfaite, insaisissable, enfermée à l'intérieur de ces mystères, et j'essaie de lui ouvrir mon âme pour en laisser pénétrer en moi la lumière." PSO, 149 (my tr.).

44. "En ce cas la foi chrétienne pourrait, sans danger de tyrannie exercée par l'Eglise sur les esprits, être placée au centre de toute la vie profane et de chacune des activités qui la composent, et tout imprégner, absolument tout, de sa lumière, Voie unique de salut pour les hommes misérables d'aujourd'hui." PSO, 153 (my tr.).

Chapter Three

1. Tr. Arthur Wills and John Petrie, *Oppression and Liberty* (London, 1958), p. 84; subsequently referred to as OAL. "Il est temps de renoncer à rêver la liberté, et de se décider à la concevoir. C'est la liberté parfaite qu'il faut s'efforcer de se présenter clairement, non pas dans l'espoir d'y atteindre, mais dans l'espoir d'atteindre une liberté moins imparfaite que n'est notre condition actuelle; car le meilleur n'est concevable que par le parfait. On ne peut se diriger que vers un idéal. L'idéal est tout aussi irréalisable que le rêve, mais à la différence du rêve, il a rapport à la réalité; il permet, à titre de limite, de ranger des situations ou réelles ou réalisables dans l'ordre de la moindre à la plus haute valeur." *Oppression et liberté* (Paris, 1955), p. 113; subsequently referred to as OEL. In addition to the very important essay quoted here, OEL contains two articles published first in 1933 and later fragments, all on the same subjects—Marxism, oppression, and the quest for social justice.

2. Tr. Arthur Wills, *The Need for Roots* (New York, 1952), p. 3; subsequently referred to as NFR. "Une obligation ne serait-elle reconnue par personne, elle ne perd rien de la plénitude de son être. Un droit qui n'est reconnu par personne n'est pas grand'chose." *L'Enracinement* (Paris, 1949), p. 9; subsequently referred to as ENR.

3. NFR, 6. "Le fait qu'un être humain possède une destinée éternelle n'impose qu'une seule obligation; c'est le respect. L'obligation n'est accomplie que si le respect est effectivement exprimé, d'une manière réelle et non fictive; il ne peut l'être que par l'intermédiaire des besoins terrestres de l'homme." ENR, 12–13.

4. NFR, 253. "Désirer la vérité, c'est désirer un contact direct avec de la réalité." ENR, 319.

5. Alfred Kazin, "The Gift," *New Yorker*, 5 July 1952, p. 60.

6. NFR, 37. "Un aiguilleur cause d'un déraillement serait mal accueilli en alléguant qu'il est de bonne foi." ENR, 53.

7. NFR, 43. "... participation réelle, active et naturelle à l'existence d'une collectivité qui conserve vivants certains trésors du passé et certains pressentiments d'avenir." ENR, 61.

8. NFR, 10. One "est blessé dans son amour du bien." ENR, 18.

9. NFR, 44. "L'argent détruit les racines partout où il pénètre, en remplaçant tous les mobiles par le désir de gagner. Il l'emporte sans peine sur les autres mobiles parce qu'il demande un effort d'attention tellement moins grand. Rien n'est si clair et si simple qu'un chiffre." ENR, 63.

10. NFR, 46. "Ce qu'on appelle aujourd'hui instruire les masses, c'est prendre cette culture moderne, élaborée dans un milieu tellement fermé, tellement taré, tellement indifférent à la vérité, en ôter tout ce qu'elle peut encore contenir d'or pur, opération qu'on nomme vulgarisation, et enfourner le résidu tel quel dans la mémoire des malheureux qui désirent apprendre, comme on donne la becquée à des oiseaux." ENR, 64–65.

11. OAL, 55. "Le mot de révolution est un mot pour lequel on tue, pour lequel on meurt, pour lequel on envoie les masses populaires à la mort, mais qui n'a aucun contenu." OEL, 79.

12. OAL, 193–94. "Le matérialisme révolutionnaire de Marx consiste à poser, d'une part que tout est réglé exclusivement par la force, d'autre part qu'un jour viendra soudain où la force sera du côté des faibles. . . . L'idée que la faiblesse comme telle, demeurant faible, peut constituer une force, n'est pas une idée nouvelle. C'est l'idée chrétienne elle-même, et la Croix en est l'illustration. Mais il s'agit d'une force d'une tout autre espèce que celle qui est maniée par les forts; c'est une force qui n'est pas de ce monde, qui est surnaturelle." OEL, 252–53.

13. OAL, 65. "Car, par un cercle sans issue, le maître est redoutable à l'esclave du fait même qu'il le redoute, et réciproquement." OEL, 91.

14. OAL, 66. "Un pouvoir . . . doit toujours tendre à s'affermir à l'intérieur au moyen de succès remportés au-dehors. . . . La lutte contre ses rivaux rallie à sa suite ses propres esclaves, qui ont l'illusion d'être intéressés à l'issue du combat. Mais pour obtenir de la part des esclaves l'obéissance et les sacrifices indispensables à un combat victorieux, le pouvoir doit se faire plus oppressif; pour être en mesure d'exercer cette oppression, il est encore plus impérieusement contraint de se tourner vers l'extérieur; et ainsi de suite." OEL, 91.

15. OAL, 115. "Les moyens de la lutte économique, publicité, luxe, corruption, investissements formidables reposant presque entièrement sur le crédit, écoulement de produits inutiles par des procédés presque violents, spéculations destinées à ruiner les entreprises rivales, tendent tous à saper les bases de notre vie économique bien plutôt qu'à les élargir." OEL, 150–51.

16. GG, 78. "La création est un acte d'amour et elle est perpétuelle. A chaque instant notre existence est amour de Dieu pour nous. Mais Dieu ne peut aimer que soi-même. Son amour pour nous est amour pour soi à travers nous. Ainsi, lui qui nous donne l'être, il aime en nous le consentement à ne pas être. Notre existence n'est faite que de son attente de notre consentement à ne pas exister. Perpétuellement, il mendie auprès de nous cette existence qu'il nous donne. Il nous la donne pour nous la mendier." PG, 41.

17. GG, 71. "Rien n'est pire que l'extrême malheur qui du dehors détruit le je, puisque dès lors on ne peut plus le détruire soi-même." PG, 35.

18. NFR, 14. "Ceux qui soumettent des masses humaines par la contrainte et la cruauté les privent à la fois de deux nourritures vitales, liberté et obéissance; car il n'est plus au pouvoir de ces masses d'accorder leur consentement intérieur à l'autorité qu'elles subissent. Ceux qui favorisent un état de choses où l'appât du gain soit le principal mobile enlèvent aux hommes l'obéissance, car le consentement qui en est le principe n'est pas une chose qui puisse se vendre." ENR, 24.

19. NFR, 86. "La situation de prostituée professionnelle constitue le degré extrême de déracinement; et pour cette maladie du déracinement, une poignée de prostituées possède un vaste pouvoir de contamination." ENR, 113.

20. WG, 159–60. "Se vider de sa fausse divinité, se nier soi-même, renoncer à être en imagination le centre du monde, discerner tous les points du monde comme étant des centres au même titre et le véritable centre comme étant hors du monde, c'est consentir au règne de la nécessité mécanique dans la matière et du libre choix au centre de chaque âme. Ce consentement est amour." AD, 148.

21. WG, 204. "Il y a harmonie parce qu'il y a unité surnaturelle entre deux contraires qui sont la nécessité et la liberté, ces deux contraires que Dieu a combinés en créant le monde et les hommes. Il y a égalité parce qu'on désire la conservation de la faculté de libre consentement en soi-même et chez l'autre. . . . Il n'y a pas d'amitié dans l'inégalité." AD, 202–3.

22. WG, 205. "L'amitié est le miracle par lequel un être humain accepte de regarder à distance et sans s'approcher l'être même qui lui est nécessaire comme une nourriture." AD, 204.

23. WG, 206. "Car on cesse de disposer l'ordre du monde en cercle autour d'un centre qui serait ici-bas. On transporte le centre au-dessus des cieux." AD, 205.

24. F. H. Sandbach, *The Stoics* (New York: Norton, 1975), p. 53.

25. "On a raison d'aimer la beauté du monde, puisqu'elle est la marque d'un échange d'amour entre le Créateur et la création. La beauté est aux choses ce que la sainteté est à l'âme." CS, 89 (my tr.).

26. "C'est de cette manière qu'à travers toutes les choses bonnes et mauvaises, indistinctement, nous devons aimer Dieu. Tant que nous aimons seulement à travers le bien, ce n'est pas Dieu que nous aimons, c'est quelque chose de terrestre que nous nommons du même nom. . . . Derrière toute réalité il y a Dieu." PSO, 37 (my tr.).

27. GG, 90. "L'obéissance est la vertu suprême." PG, 51.

28. GG, 91. ". . . faire seulement, en fait d'actes de vertu, ceux dont on ne peut pas s'empêcher, ceux qu'on ne peut pas ne pas faire." PG, 52.

29. GG, 92. ". . . détachement des fruits de l'action. . . . Agir, non *pour* un objet, mais *par* une nécessité. Je ne peux pas faire autrement. Ce n'est pas une action, mais une sorte de passivité. Action non agissante." PG, 52.

30. SWL, 36. "Pour leur rendre la forme humaine, leur soeur doit filer et coudre pour eux six chemises en anémones blanches, et ne point parler tant que durera le travail. Elle met six ans à faire ces chemises. Son silence la met en grand péril, car elle est en butte à des accusations auxquelles elle ne peut répondre. Enfin, quand elle est sur le point d'être envoyée au supplice, on voit les cygnes apparaître, elle jette sur eux les chemises d'anémones et ils reprennent la forme humaine; elle est alors sauvée, car elle peut désormais se justifier." VSW, 80.

31. SWL, 37. "Le sacrifice est l'acceptation de la douleur, le refus d'obéir à l'animal en soi, et la volonté de racheter les hommes souffrants par la souffrance volontaire. Chaque saint a répandu l'eau; chaque saint a refusé tout bonheur qui le séparerait des souffrances des hommes." VSW, 82.

32. The essay "La personne et le sacré" was written in London in 1942 or 1943. It appears in French in *Ecrits de Londres,* pp. 11–44, and in English as "Human Personality" in *The Simone Weil Reader,* edited by George A. Panichas (New York, 1977), pp. 313–39; subsequently referred to as SWR.

33. SWR, 318. "Ce qui est sacré, bien loin que ce soit la personne, c'est ce qui, dans un être humain, est impersonnel. . . . Si un enfant fait une addition, et s'il se trompe, l'erreur porte le cachet de sa personne. S'il procède d'une manière parfaitement correcte, sa personne est absente de toute l'opération. La perfection est impersonnelle. La personne en nous, c'est la part en nous de l'erreur et du péché. Tout l'effort des mystiques a toujours visé à obtenir qu'il n'y ait plus dans leur âme aucune partie qui dise 'je.' " EL, 16–17.

34. NFR, 17. "Dans la mesure où il est réellement possible qu'un enfant, fils de valet de ferme, soit un jour ministre, dans cette mesure il doit être réellement possible qu'un enfant, fils de ministre, soit un jour valet de ferme." ENR, 27.

35. NFR, 21. "Il faut que le châtiment soit un honneur, que non seulement il efface la honte du crime, mais qu'il soit regardé comme une éducation supplémentaire qui oblige à un plus grand degré de dévouement au bien public." ENR, 33.

36. SWR, 335–36. "Ceux qui sont devenus étrangers au bien au point de chercher à répandre le mal autour d'eux ne peuvent être réintégrés dans le bien que par l'infliction du mal. Il faut leur en infliger jusqu'à ce que s'éveille au fond d'eux-mêmes la voix parfaitement innocente qui dit avec étonnement: 'Pourquoi me fait-on du mal?' Cette partie innocente de l'âme du criminel, il faut qu'elle reçoive de la nourriture et qu'elle croisse, jusqu'à ce qu'elle se constitue elle-même un tribunal à l'intérieur de l'âme, pour juger les crimes passés, pour les condamner, et ensuite, avec le secours de la grâce, pour les pardonner. L'opération du châtiment est alors achevée; le coupable est réintégré dans le bien, et doit être publiquement et so-lennellement réintégré dans la cité. Le châtiment n'est pas autre chose que cela. Même la peine capitale, bien qu'elle exclue la réintégration dans la cité au sens littéral, ne doit pas être autre chose. Le châtiment est unique-ment un procédé pour fournir du bien pur à des hommes qui ne le désirent pas; l'art de punir est l'art d'éveiller chez les criminels le désir du bien pur par la douleur ou même par la mort." EL, 40.

37. WG, 156. "Rien n'est plus affreux que le spectacle si fréquent d'un accusé, n'ayant dans la situation où il se trouve aucune ressource au monde sinon sa parole, mais incapable de manier la parole à cause de son origine sociale et de son manque de culture, abattu par la culpabilité, le malheur et la peur, balbutiant devant des juges qui n'écoutent pas et qui l'interrompent en faisant ostentation d'un langage raffiné." AD, 144.

38. WG, 155. "L'important est . . . que toute l'organisation de la justice pénale ait pour fin d'obtenir des magistrats et de leurs aides, pour l'accusé, l'attention et le respect dû par tout homme à quiconque se trouve à sa discrétion, et de l'accusé le consentement à la peine infligée, ce consentement dont le Christ innocent a donné le parfait modèle." AD, 143–44.

39. NFR, 168. "Toute autre nation avait à la rigueur le droit de se tailler un Empire, mais non pas la France; pour la même raison qui a fait de la souveraineté temporelle du pape un scandale aux yeux de la chrétienté. Quand on assume, comme a fait la France en 1789, la fonction de penser pour l'univers, de définir pour lui la justice, on ne devient pas propriétaire de chair humaine." ENR, 214.

40. NFR, 160. ". . . l'imitation de la passion du Christ portée à l'échelle nationale." ENR, 204.

41. NFR, 179. "Si l'on incline à désobéir, mais qu'on soit arrêté par l'excès du danger, on est impardonnable, selon les cas, ou bien d'avoir songé à désobéir, ou bien de ne l'avoir pas fait. Au reste, toutes les fois qu'on n'est pas rigoureusement obligé de désobéir, on est rigoureusement obligé d'obéir. . . . L'ordre public doit être tenu pour plus sacré que la propriétée privée." ENR, 227–28.

42. NFR, 147. "Il y a eu une nation jadis qui s'est crue sainte, et cela lui a très mal réussi; et à ce sujet il est bien étrange de penser que les Pharasiens étaient les résistants, dans cette nation, et les publicains les collaborateurs, et de se rappeler quels étaient les rapports du Christ avec les uns et les autres." ENR, 188.

43. NFR, 157. "Le gouvernement qui surgira en France après la libération du territoire sera devant le triple danger causé par ce goût du sang, ce complexe de mendicité, cette incapacité d'obéir." ENR, 200.

44. "Le mouvement français de Londres a précisément le degré qui convient de caractère officiel pour que les directives envoyées par lui contiennent le stimulant attaché à des ordres, sans pourtant ternir l'espèce d'ivresse lucide et pure qui accompagne le libre consentement au sacrifice. Il en résulte pour lui des possibilités et des responsabilités immenses." ENR, 258–59 (my tr.).

45. NFR, 219. "Quatre obstacles surtout nous séparent d'une forme de civilisation susceptible de valoir quelque chose. Notre conception fausse de la grandeur; la dégradation du sentiment de la justice; notre idolatrie de l'argent; et' l'absence en nous d'inspiration religieuse." ENR, 277.

46. "La fonction spirituelle du travail physique est la contemplation des choses, la contemplation de la nature." CS, 29 (my tr.).

47. NFR, 300. "Le travail physique est une mort quotidienne." ENR, 378.

48. NFR, 295. "Le travail physique consenti est, après la mort consentie, la forme la plus parfaite de la vertu d'obéissance." ENR, 372.

49. NFR, 300. "Le travail et la mort, si l'homme les subit en consentant à les subir, constituent un transport dans le bien de l'obéissance à Dieu." ENR, 377.

50. NFR, 302. "Il est facile de définir la place que doit occuper le travail physique dans une vie sociale bien organisée. Il doit en être le centre spirituel." ENR, 380.

51. "Le travail manuel est ou bien une servitude dégradante pour l'âme, ou bien un sacrifice. Dans le cas du travail des champs, le lien avec l'Eucharistie, si seulement il est senti, suffit pour en faire un sacrifice." PSO, 25 (my tr.).

52. "Il faudrait . . . trouver et définir pour chaque aspect de la vie sociale son lien spécifique avec le Christ. . . . Ainsi comme la vie religieuse est répartie en ordres qui correspondent à des vocations, de même la vie social apparaîtrait comme un édifice de vocations distinctes convergeant dans le Christ." PSO, 33 (my tr.).

53. "Il s'agit de transformer, dans la plus large mesure possible, la vie quotidienne elle-même en une métaphore à signification divine, en une parabole." PSO, 24 (my tr.).

Chapter Four

1. NFR, 234. "Il y a un point de grandeur où le génie créateur de beauté, le génie révélateur de vérité, l'héroisme et la sainteté sont indiscernables." ENR, 295.

2. WG, 170. "L'artiste, le savant, le penseur, le contemplatif doivent pour admirer réellement l'univers percer cette pellicule d'irréalité qui le voile et en fait pour presque tous les hommes, à presque tous les moments de leur vie, un rêve ou un décor de théâtre." AD, 161.

3. GG, 204. "Le beau est le nécessaire, qui, tout en demeurant conforme à sa loi propre et à elle seule, obéit au bien." PG, 149.

4. "La grande douleur de la vie humaine, c'est que regarder et manger soient deux opérations différentes." AD, 156 (my tr.).

5. GG, 206. "Le regard et l'attente, c'est l'attitude qui correspond au beau." PG, 150–51.

6. SWR, 333. "La beauté est le mystère suprême d'ici-bas. C'est un éclat qui sollicite l'attention, mais ne lui fournit aucun mobile pour durer. La beauté promet toujours et ne donne jamais rien; elle suscite une faim, mais il n'y a pas en elle de nourriture pour la partie de l'âme qui essaie ici-bas de se rassasier; elle n'a de nourriture que pour la partie de l'âme qui regarde. Elle suscite le désir, car on ne cherche pas d'expédients pour sortir du tourment délicieux qu'elle inflige, le désir peu à peu se transforme en amour, et il se forme un germe de la faculté d'attention gratuite et pure." EL, 37.

7. SWR, 334. "L'éclat de la beauté est répandu sur le malheur par la lumière de l'esprit de justice et d'amour, qui seul permet à une pensée humaine de regarder et de reproduire le malheur tel qu'il est." EL, 37.

8. WG, 123–24. "Dieu a créé . . . des êtres capables d'amour à toutes les distances possibles. Lui-même est allé, parce que nul autre ne pouvait le faire, à la distance maximum, la distance infinie. Cette distance infinie entre Dieu et Dieu, déchirement suprême, douleur dont aucune autre n'approche, merveille de l'amour, c'est la crucifixion. Rien ne peut être plus loin de Dieu que ce qui a été fait malédiction. Ce déchirement par-dessus lequel l'amour suprême met le lien de la suprême union résonne perpétuellement à travers l'univers, au fond du silence, comme deux notes

séparées et fondues, comme une harmonie pure et déchirante. C'est cela la Parole de Dieu. La création tout entière n'en est que la vibration. Quand la musique humaine dans sa plus grande pureté nous perce l'âme, c'est cela que nous entendons à travers elle." AD, 106.

9. WG, 169. "Les oeuvres d'art qui ne sont pas des reflets justes et purs de la beauté du monde, des ouvertures directes pratiquées sur elle, ne sont pas à proprement parler belles; elles ne sont pas de premier ordre; leurs auteurs peuvent avoir beaucoup de talent, mais non pas authentiquement du génie. C'est le cas de beaucoup d'oeuvres d'art parmi les plus célèbres et les plus vantées. Tout véritable artiste a eu un contact réel, direct, immédiat avec la beauté du monde, ce contact qui est quelque chose comme un sacrement. Dieu a inspiré toute oeuvre d'art de premier ordre, le sujet en fût-il mille fois profane; il n'a inspiré aucune des autres. En revanche, parmis les autres, l'éclat de la beauté qui recouvre certaines pourrait bien être un éclat diabolique." AD, 159–60.

10. "On ne peut pas passer par le bien sans passer par le beau." CS, 17 (my tr.).

11. GG, 207. "En tout ce qui suscite chez nous le sentiment pur et authentique du beau, il y a réellement présence de Dieu. . . . Le contact avec le beau est au plein sens du mot un sacrement." PG, 151.

12. WG, 130. "Si parfois, dans une oeuvre d'art, elle [la matière] apparaît presque aussi belle que dans la mer, les montagnes ou les fleurs, c'est que la lumière de Dieu a empli l'artiste." AD, 114.

13. ". . . comme le crayon est appuyé par moi sur le papier." CS, 16 (my tr.).

14. OSN, 133. "Si un artiste essaie d'imiter soit une chose sensible, soit un phénomène psychologique, un sentiment, etc., il fait oeuvre médiocre. Dans la création d'une oeuvre d'art de tout premier ordre, l'attention de l'artiste est orientée vers le silence et le vide; de ce silence et de ce vide descend une inspiration qui se développe en paroles ou en formes. . . . (Pas d'intention particulière. Le poète qui met tel mot pour tel effet est un poète médiocre.)" SG, 130–31.

15. NFR, 284. "Tous les effets, toutes les résonances, toutes les évocations susceptibles d'être amenés par la présence de tel mot à telle place, répondent au même degré, c'est-à-dire parfaitement, à l'inspiration du poète. Il en est de même pour tous les arts. C'est ainsi que le poète imite Dieu." ENR, 357–58.

16. ". . . nous rendre l'espace et le temps sensibles. Nous fabriquer un espace, un temps humains, faits par l'homme, qui pourtant soient *le* temps, *l'*espace." C, 1:14, italics hers (my tr.).

17. WG, 168. "L'art est une tentative pour transporter dans une quantité finie de matière modelée par l'homme une image de la beauté infinie de l'univers entier. Si la tentative est réussie, cette portion de

matière ne doit pas cacher l'univers, mais au contraire en révéler la réalité tout autour." AD, 159.

18. "La violence du temps déchire l'âme; par la déchirure entre l'éternité." C, 1:51 (my tr.).

19. WG, 171. "Mais c'est la beauté du monde, la beauté universelle vers laquelle se dirige le désir. Cette espèce de transfert est ce qu'exprime toute la littérature qui entoure l'amour, depuis les métaphores et les comparaisons les plus anciennes, les plus usées de la poésie jusqu'aux analyses subtiles de Proust. Le désir d'aimer dans un être humain la beauté du monde est essentiellement le désir de l'Incarnation." AD, 163.

20. OSN, 160. "Le bien fictif est ennuyeux et plat. Le mal fictif est varié, intéressant, attachant, profond, plein de séductions." "Morale et littérature," Les Cahiers du Sud, no. 263 (January 1944):40 (under the pseudonym of Emile Novis).

21. OSN, 162. They give us "sous la forme de la fiction quelque chose d'équivalent à l'épaisseur même de la réalité" because they are "hors de la fiction et nous en sortent." Ibid., p. 42.

22. OSN, 165. They are able to "faire pousser des ailes contre la pesanteur." Ibid., p. 45.

23. NFR, 25. ". . . derrière le privilège sacré de l'art pour l'art. . . . Il n'y a dès lors aucun motif de mettre de tels livres derrière la barrière intouchable de l'art pour l'art, et d'emprisonner un garçon qui jette quelqu'un hors d'un train en marche." ENR, 38. In Les Caves du Vatican Gide's protagonist, Lafcadio, believes the most creative moral act is "the gratuitous act" (l'acte gratuit). He commits such an act when he pushes a man out of a moving train.

24. NFR, 25. "On pourrait tout aussi bien réclamer les privilèges de l'art pour l'art en faveur du crime. Autrefois les surréalistes n'en étaient pas loin." ENR, 38.

25. OSN, 161. "Comme les lecteurs ne constituent pas une espèce animale particulière, comme ceux qui lisent sont les mêmes qui accomplissent quantité d'autres fonctions." "Morale et littérature," p. 41.

26. OSN, 167. ". . . l'ivresse de la licence totale. . . . Rejetant toute considération de valeur, il se livre à l'immédiat. . . . Le sac des villes n'a pas toujours eu d'équivalent littéraire. Le surréalisme est un tel équivalent." "Responsabilités de la littérature," Les Cahiers du Sud, no. 310 (1951):428.

27. OSN, 168. ". . . des états d'âme non orientés." Ibid., p. 429.

28. OSN, 163. "Comme la maturité du génie est la conformité au vrai rapport du bien et du mal, l'oeuvre qui correspond à la maturité du génie démoniaque est le silence." "Morale et littérature," p. 43.

29. SG, 11–42; tr. Mary McCarthy, "The Iliad," or the Poem of Force (Wallingford, Pa.: Pendle Hill, 1956), subsequently referred to as IPF.

30. IPF, 3. "Quand elle s'exerce jusqu'au bout, elle fait de l'homme une chose au sens le plus littéral, car elle en fait un cadavre." SG, 11.

31. IPF, 14. "C'est ainsi que ceux à qui la force est prêtée par le sort périssent pour y trop compter." SG, 22.

32. IPF, 19. "La violence écrase ceux qu'elle touche. Elle finit par apparaître extérieure à celui qui la manie comme à celui qui la souffre; alors naît l'idée d'un destin sous lequel les bourreaux et les victimes sont pareillement innocents, les vainqueurs et les vaincus frères dans la même misère." SG, 26.

33. IPF, 15. "Ce châtiment d'une rigueur géométrique, qui punit automatiquement l'abus de la force, fut l'objet premier de la méditation chez les Grecs." SG, 22.

34. IPF, 15. "Nous ne sommes géomètres que devant la matière; les Grecs furent d'abord géomètres dans l'apprentissage de la vertu." SG, 23.

35. IPF, 27. ". . . parsemés çà et là, des moments lumineux; moments brefs et divins où les hommes ont une âme." SG, 33.

36. IPF, 29. ". . . l'amitié qui monte au coeur des ennemis mortels. . . . Elle efface par un miracle encore plus grand la distance entre bienfaiteur et suppliant, entre vainqueur et vaincu. . . . Ces moments de grâce sont rares dans l'*Iliade,* mais ils suffisent pour faire sentir avec un extrême regret ce que la violence fait et fera périr." SG, 35.

37. OSN, 121. "Nous n'avons naturellement la notion que des réalités de ce monde. Le passé est du réel à notre niveau, mais qui n'est aucunement à notre portée, vers lequel nous ne pouvons pas faire même un pas, vers lequel nous pouvons seulement nous orienter pour qu'une émanation de lui vienne à nous. C'est pourquoi le passé est la meilleure image des réalités éternelles, surnaturelles. (La joie, la beauté du souvenir tient peut-être à cela.) Proust avait entrevu cela." SG, 117.

38. NFR, 143. "Alexandre pleurait, dit-on, de n'avoir à conquérir que le globe terrestre. Corneille croyait apparemment que le Christ était descendu sur terre pour combler cette lacune." ENR, 183.

39. NFR, 281–82. ". . . à la fois atroce et stupide, également révoltante pour l'intelligence et pour le coeur. Il faut être bien sensible à la sonorité des mots pour regarder ce prélat courtisan comme un grand esprit." ENR, 354.

40. NFR, 188. "La beauté de son oeuvre est une marque suffisamment évidente d'authenticité." ENR, 238.

41. NFR, 235. "L'*Iliade,* les tragédies d'Eschyle et celles de Sophocle portent la marque évidente que les poètes qui ont fait cela étaient dans l'état de sainteté. . . . Monteverdi, Bach, Mozart furent des êtres purs dans leur vie comme dans leur oeuvre." ENR, 196.

42. NFR, 175. "Les romantiques furent des enfants qui s'ennuyaient parce qu'il n'y avait plus devant eux la perspective d'une ascension sociale

illimitée. Ils cherchèrent la gloire littéraire comme produit de remplacement." ENR, 223.

43. NFR, 235. "Du point de vue purement poétique, sans tenir compte de rien d'autre, il est infiniment préférable d'avoir composé le Cantique de saint François d'Assise, ce joyau de beauté parfaite, plutôt que toute l'oeuvre de Victor Hugo." ENR, 296.

44. Weil does not specifically name which of the famous "Messieurs" of Port-Royal she has in mind.

45. NFR, 96. "Les pensées qui se rapportent au pressentiment de cette vocation, et qui sont éparses chez Rousseau, George Sand, Tolstoi, Proudhon, Marx, dans les encycliques des papes, et ailleurs, sont les seules pensées originales de notre temps, les seules que nous n'ayons pas empruntées aux Grecs." ENR, 125.

Chapter Five

1. NFR, 262. "L'investigation scientifique n'est qu'une forme de la contemplation religieuse." ENR, 329.

2. OSN, 8. "Cette nécessité tient au temps lui-même et consiste en ce qu'il est dirigé, en sorte que, quoi qu'il arrive, le sens d'une transformation n'est jamais indifférent." *Sur la science* (Paris, 1966), p. 128; subsequently referred to as SLS.

3. OSN, 9–10. "La science classique . . . devait dès lors se croire capable, par les calculs, les mesures, les équivalences numériques, de lire, à travers tous les phénomènes qui se produisent dans l'univers, de simples variations de l'énergie et de l'entropie conformes à une loi simple." SLS, 130.

4. OSN, 10. "Elle . . . cherche à lire à travers toutes les apparences cette nécessité inexorable qui fait du monde un monde où nous ne comptons pas." SLS, 131.

5. Anne Reynaud, *Leçons de philosophie* (Paris, 1959), pp. 122–23. Tr. Hugh Price, *Lectures on Philosophy* (London, 1978), p. 125.

6. OSN, 24. "Discontinu, nombre, petitesse, c'est assez pour faire surgir l'atome, et l'atome est revenu parmi nous avec son cortège inséparable, à savoir le hasard et la probabilité." SLS, 150.

7. OSN, 22. "La science du XXe siècle, c'est la science classique après qu'on lui a retiré quelque chose. Retiré, non pas ajouté. On n'y a apporté aucune notion, et surtout on n'y a pas ajouté ce dont l'absence en faisait un désert, le rapport au bien. On en a retiré l'analogie entre les lois de la nature et les conditions du travail, c'est-à-dire le principe même; c'est l'hypothèse des quanta qui l'a ainsi décapitée." SLS, 147.

8. OSN, 23, 22. "La formule de Planck, faite d'une constante dont on n'imagine pas la provenance et d'un nombre qui correspond à une probabilité, n'a aucun rapport avec aucune pensée. Comment est-ce qu'on

la justifie? On en fonde la légitimité sur la quantité des calculs, des expériences issues des calculs, des applications techniques procédant de ces expériences qui ont réussi grâce à cette formule. Planck lui-même n'allègue rien d'autre. Pareille chose une fois admise, la physique devient un ensemble de signes et de nombres combinés en des formules qui sont contrôlées par les applications. . . . Le rapport qui est le principe de cette science est simplement le rapport entre des formules algébriques vides de signification et la technique." SLS, 149, 147.

9. OSN, 61. "La notion de probabilité, séparée de celle de nécessité . . . n'est plus que le résumé des statistiques." SLS, 204.

10. OSN, 30. "C'est là le point crucial dans tout examen critique de la théorie des quanta. . . . Planck a pu faire tout un livre . . . sur les rapports de la science contemporaine et de la philosophie, sans y faire même une lointaine allusion." SLS, 158.

11. OSN, 62. "Tout effort humain est orienté." SLS, 205.

12. OSN, 62–63. "Les savants de la période classique avaient une représentation de la vérité scientifique certes fort défectueuse, mais ils en avaient une; et ceux d'aujourd'hui n'ont dans l'esprit aucune chose, fût-elle vague, lointaine, arbitraire, impossible, vers laquelle ils puissent se tourner la nommant vérité. . . . Dès que la vérité disparaît, l'utilité aussitôt prend sa place. . . . Mais cette utilité, l'intelligence n'a plus alors qualité pour la définir ni pour en juger, elle a seulement licence de la servir." SLS, 205–7.

13. OSN, 31–32. "Ce qui est négligé est toujours aussi grand que le monde, exactement aussi grand, car un physicien néglige toute la différence entre une chose qui se produit sous ses yeux et un système parfaitement clos, parfaitement défini qu'il conçoit dans son esprit et représente sur le papier par des images et des signes; et cette différence, c'est le monde même. . . . On néglige le monde, parce qu'il le faut, et, ne pouvant appliquer la mathématique aux choses à un prix moindre, on l'applique au prix d'une erreur infinie." SLS, 160–61.

14. OSN, 32, 34. "En un sens, une observation, une expérience sont exactement pour un physicien ce qu'est une figure pour un géomètre. . . . Dans toute la mesure où la notion de nécessité joue un rôle en physique, la physique est essentiellement l'application de la mathématique à la nature au prix d'une erreur infinie." SLS, 161, 163.

15. NFR, 69. "La plupart ignoreront toujours que presque toutes nos actions, simples ou savamment combinées, sont des applications de notions géométriques, et que la nécessité géométrique est celle même à laquelle nous sommes soumis en fait, comme créatures enfermées dans l'espace et le temps." ENR, 93.

16. OSN, 35, 41. "Que la droite pure, l'angle pur, le triangle pur, soient des ouvrages de l'attention qui fait effort en se détachant des ap-

parences sensibles et des actions, nous en avons conscience toutes les fois que nous pensons ces notions. . . . Nous refusons le monde pour penser mathématiquement, et à l'issue de cet effort de renoncement le monde nous est donné comme par surcroît, au prix, il est vrai, d'une erreur infinie, mais réellement donnée. Par ce renoncement aux choses, par ce contact avec la réalité qui l'accompagne comme un récompense gratuite, la géométrie est une image de la vertu. Pour poursuivre le bien aussi nous nous détournons des choses, et reçevons le monde en récompense; comme la droite tracée à la craie est ce qu'on trace avec la craie en pensant à la droite, de même l'acte de vertu est ce qu'on accomplit en aimant Dieu, et, comme la droite tracée, il enferme une erreur infinie." SLS, 165, 174.

17. Quoted in OSN, 80. "C'est à partir de cela que se fait la production des choses, et leur destruction est un retour à cela, conforme à la nécessité; car les choses subissent un châtiment et une expiation les unes de la part des autres à cause de leurs injustices selon l'ordre du temps." SLS, 276.

18. OSN, 16. "Aussi la science classique n'est-elle pas belle; ni elle ne touche le coeur ni elle ne contient une sagesse. . . . Il en était tout autrement chez les Grecs. Hommes heureux, en qui l'amour, l'art et la science n'étaient que trois aspects à peine différents du même mouvement de l'âme vers le bien." SLS, 139.

19. OSN, 19. "Au lieu du rapport entre le désir et les conditions de l'accomplissement, la science grecque a pour objet le rapport entre l'ordre et les conditions de l'ordre." SLS, 143.

20. OSN, 21. "La science grecque, elle, considère les mêmes conditions que la science classique, mais elle a égard à une aspiration toute autre, l'aspiration à contempler dans les apparences sensibles une image du bien." SLS, 146.

21. OSN, 79–84: "Du fondement d'une science nouvelle," in SLS, 275–81.

22. NFR, 261. ". . . l'étude de la beauté du monde." ENR, 329.

23. Tr. Richard Rees, Seventy Letters (London, 1965), pp. 117–18. "La pureté d'âme était leur unique souci; 'imiter Dieu' en était le secret; l'étude de la mathématique aidait à imiter Dieu pour autant qu'on regardait l'univers comme soumis aux lois mathématiques, ce qui faisait du géomètre un imitateur du législateur suprême." SLS, 219–20.

24. OSN, 79. "La délivrance est de lire la limite et la relation dans toutes les apparences sensibles, sans exception, aussi clairement et immédiatement qu'un sens dans un texte imprimé. La signification d'une science véritable est de constituer une préparation à la délivrance." SLS, 275.

25. OSN, 83. "Jusqu'ici, la science n'a pas formulé un troisième principe, mais il est clair qu'il faut un troisième qui balance la dégradation

de l'énergie, car autrement l'entropie maximum serait déjà atteinte partout et tout serait immobile et mort." SLS, 280.
   26. SWL, 200. VSW, 404–5.
   27. WG, 109. "La contemplation de sa propre bêtise est plus utile peut-être même que celle du péché." AD, 89–90.
   28. WG, 112. "La cause est toujours qu'on a voulu être actif; on a voulu chercher. . . . Les biens les plus précieux ne doivent pas être cherchés, mais attendus." AD, 92–93.
   29. WG, 113. "Il y a pour chaque exercice scolaire une manière spécifique d'attendre la vérité avec désir et sans se permettre de la chercher." AD, 94.

Chapter Six

   1. Camus also included several other works by Weil in this collection.
   2. Albert Camus, *Oeuvres complètes* (Paris, 1959), 2:1700.
   3. Albert Béguin, "La Raideur et la grâce: à propos de Simone Weil," *Témoignage chrétien,* 2 December 1949.
   4. Gabriel Marcel, "Les Carnets d'un Don Quichotte," *Liens,* March 1954, pp. 8–9.
   5. François Mauriac, "Bucolique," *Le Figaro,* 8 May 1950, p. 1.
   6. Georges Bataille, "La Victoire militaire et la banqueroute de la morale qui maudit: Simone Weil, *L'Enracinement,*" *Critique,* September 1949, pp. 789–803.
   7. Marie-Magdeleine Davy, *Introduction au message de Simone Weil* (Paris, 1954).
   8. Joseph-Marie Perrin and Gustave Thibon, *Simone Weil telle que nous l'avons connue* (Paris, 1952).
   9. *The Need for Roots* (New York, 1952), p. vi.
   10. Graham Greene, "Simone Weil," *New Statesman and Nation* 42 (6 October 1951):372–74.
   11. Kenneth Rexroth, "The Dialectic of Agony," *Nation* 184, no. 2 (12 January 1957):42.
   12. Ibid., p. 43.
   13. Dwight MacDonald, "A Formula to Give a War-Torn Society Fresh Roots," *New York Times Book Review,* July 6, 1952, p. 6.
   14. Alfred Kazin, "The Gift," *New Yorker,* 5 July 1952, pp. 57–60.
   15. E. W. F. Tomlin, *Simone Weil* (New Haven, 1954).
   16. Simone Pétrement, *La vie de Simone Weil* (Paris, 1973).
   17. Janet Patricia Little, *Simone Weil* (London, 1973).
   18. Richard Rees, *Simone Weil: A Sketch for a Portrait* (London, 1966).
   19. George Abbott White, *Simone Weil: Interpretations of a Life* (Amherst, 1981).

20. Malcolm Muggeridge, "Agonies and Ecstasies," *Observer*, 22 September 1968, p. 31.

21. "Etre poussé par Dieu vers le prochain comme le crayon est appuyé par moi sur le papier." CS, 16 (my tr.).

Selected Bibliography

PRIMARY SOURCES

(Note: French books are published in Paris unless otherwise stated. Primary sources are arranged chronologically.)

La Pesanteur et la grâce. Plon Collection "L'Epi," 1947 (Plon's Collection "Le Monde en 10–18" edition quoted in text). Translated by Arthur Wills as *Gravity and Grace*. New York: G. P. Putnam's Sons, 1952.

L'Enracinement, prélude à une déclaration des devoirs envers l'être humain. Gallimard Collection "Espoir," 1949 (Gallimard's Collection "Idées" edition quoted in text; contains materials not printed in original edition). Translated by Arthur Wills as *The Need for Roots*. New York: G. P. Putnam's Sons, 1952.

Attente de Dieu. La Colombe, Editions du Vieux Colombier, 1950 (Fayard's 1966 "Livre de poche chrétien" edition quoted in text). Translated by Emma Craufurd as *Waiting for God*. New York: G. P. Putnam's Son's, 1951.

La Connaissance surnaturelle. Gallimard Collection "Espoir," 1950. Included in Richard Rees's translation *First and Last Notebooks*. London: Oxford University Press, 1970.

Cahiers, I. Plon Collection "L'Epi," 1951 (volumes 2 and 3 published by Plon respectively in 1953 and 1956). Translated by Arthur Wills as *the Notebooks of Simone Weil*. 2 vols. New York: G. P. Putnam's Sons, 1956.

La Condition ouvrière. Gallimard Collection "Espoir," 1951 (Gallimard's Collection "Idées" edition quoted in text). Portions translated and included in Richard Rees's *Simone Weil: Seventy Letters*. London: Oxford University Press, 1965.

Intuitions préchrétiennes. La Colombe, Editions du Vieux Colombier, 1951. Translated by Elisabeth Chase Geissbuhler as *Intimations of Christianity Among the Ancient Greeks*. London: Routledge & Kegan Paul, 1957.

Lettre à un religieux. Gallimard Collection "Espoir," 1951. Translated by Arthur Wills as *Letter to a Priest*. New York: G. P. Putnam's Sons, 1954.

La Source grecque. Gallimard Collection "Espoir," 1953. Major portions translated and included in *Intimations of Christianity* and Richard Rees's

On Science, Necessity, and the Love of God. London: Oxford University Press, 1968.

Oppression et liberté. Gallimard Collection "Espoir," 1955. Translated by Arthur Wills and John Petrie as *Oppression and Liberty.* London: Routledge & Kegan Paul, 1958. Reprint. Amherst: University of Massachusetts Press, 1973.

Ecrits de Londres et dernières lettres. Gallimard Collection "Espoir," 1960. Portions translated and included in Richard Rees's *Simone Weil: Selected Essays, 1934–1943.* London: Oxford University Press, 1962.

Pensées sans ordre concernant l'amour de Dieu. Gallimard Collection "Espoir," 1962. Portions translated and included in *Seventy Letters* and *The Simone Weil Reader.* Edited by George A. Panichas. New York: David McKay, 1977.

Sur la science. Gallimard Collection "Espoir," 1966. Except for Weil's thesis, *Science et perception dans Descartes,* and a few letters, these materials are translated by Richard Rees and included in *On Science, Necessity, and the Love of God.*

SECONDARY SOURCES

1. Books

Cabaud, Jacques. *Simone Weil: A Fellowship in Love.* New York: Channel Press, 1965. Well-documented, well-written biography, the best available in English. Major weakness is tendency to give excessively lengthy résumés and interpretations of Weil's writings.

―――. *Simone Weil à New York et à Londres.* Plon, 1967. Contains important material (not included in earlier biography) on the last months of Weil's life, most of which is also covered in Pétrement.

Davy, Marie-Magdeleine. *Introduction au message de Simone Weil.* Plon Collection "L'Epi," 1954. An attempt to correct what she finds to be a Roman Catholic interpretation of Weil's "message."

Heidsieck, François. *Simone Weil.* Seghers, Philosophes de tous les temps, 1965. Intelligent presentation of major concerns of Weil's philosophy, although limited in scope. Includes section of extensive quotations, primarily from religious writings.

Little, Janet Patricia. *Simone Weil.* London: Grant & Cutler, 1973; supplement, 1980. The definitive bibliography, indispensable tool in sorting out the confusing jumble of Weil's published work.

Perrin, Joseph-Marie, and Thibon, Gustave. *Simone Weil telle que nous l'avons connue.* La Colombe, Editions du Vieux Colombier, 1952. Translated by Emma Craufurd as *Simone Weil as We Knew Her.* London: Routledge & Kegan Paul, 1953. Extremely important document because of close relationship both authors had with Weil near the end of her life. Thibon's essay is especially perceptive.

Pétrement, Simone. *La vie de Simone Weil, avec des lettres et d'autres textes inédits.* 2 vols. Fayard, 1973. Translated by Raymond Rosenthal as *Simone Weil: A Life.* New York: Pantheon, 1976. The definitive biography. Author's personal acquaintance with Weil is almost always an asset, despite occasional tendencies toward canonizing. Well written, reveals a sound grasp of Weil's philosophical insights. The English version, however, is lamentably translated and severely edited.

Rees, Richard. *Simone Weil: A Sketch for a Portrait.* London: Oxford University Press, 1966. Succeeds in focusing on Weil's thought without excessive veneration of her life. Possibly the best general study of her writings.

Reynaud, Anne, ed. *Leçons de philosophie, Roanne, 1933–34.* Plon, 1959. Translated by Hugh Price as *Lectures on Philosophy.* London: Cambridge University Press, 1978. Notes from Weil's philosophy class at Roanne by one of her students. Interesting insight into Weil as a teacher. Not to be taken, of course, as a text purely *by* Simone Weil.

Tomlin, Eric Walter Frederick. *Simone Weil.* New Haven: Yale University Press, 1954. Very useful brief introduction. Well-written and well-conceived analysis. Limited only by brevity and date (too early to take into account several important works published subsequently).

White, George Abbott, ed. *Simone Weil: Interpretations of a Life.* Amherst: University of Massachusetts Press, 1981. An extremely valuable collection of essays for their freshly original interpretations. Admirably free of the academic specialist's jargon. Emphasis on implications of Weil's thought in the world of action.

2. Chapters, Articles, and Reviews

Brée, Germaine. "A Stranger in this World." *Saturday Review* 48 (20 February 1965):26–27. Brief but interesting review of Cabaud's biography.

Camus, Albert. Preface to *L'Enracinement.* Reprinted in Camus's *Oeuvres complètes.* Pléiade edition, 1959, 2:1700–2. Evidence of Weil's importance to Camus.

Cohen, Robert S. "Parallels and the Possibility of Influence between Simone Weil's *Waiting for God* and Samuel Beckett's *Waiting for Godot.*" *Modern Drama* (February 1964):425–36.

Eliot, T. S. Preface to *The Need for Roots.* New York: G. P. Putnam's Sons, 1952, pp. v–xii. Interesting glimpse at this important Christian poet's attitude toward Weil.

Greene, Graham. "Simone Weil." *New Statesman and Nation* 42 (6 October 1951):372–74. Also in *Collected Essays.* London: Bodley Head, 1969,

p. 1074. Review of *Waiting for God*. Very hard on the unorthodox religious thought of Weil.

Kazin, Alfred. "The Gift." *New Yorker*, 5 July 1952, pp. 57–60. Also in *The Inmost Leaf: A Selection of Essays*. New York: Harcourt, Brace, & Co., 1955, pp. 208–13. Good review article on *The Need for Roots*.

MacDonald, Dwight. "A Formula to Give a War-Torn Society Fresh Roots." *New York Times Book Review*, 6 July 1952, p. 6. Intelligent, fair-minded review of *The Need for Roots*. Avoids blind adoration, yet gives a sensitive appreciation of the strengths of this text.

Merton, Thomas. "Pacifism and Resistance in Simone Weil." In *Faith and Violence: Christian Teaching and Christian Practice*. Notre Dame: University of Notre Dame Press, 1968, pp. 76–84. Fine study of nonviolence in Simone Weil.

Peyre, Henri. "Simone Weil." *Massachusetts Review* 6 (1964):504–14. Highly intelligent and sensitive essay.

Pierce, Roy. "Simone Weil: Sociology, Utopia, and Faith." In *Contemporary French Political Thought*. London: Oxford University Press, 1966, pp. 89–121. Excellent piece of scholarship. Emphasis on Weil's methodology of sociopolitical analysis and theoretical implications of her philosophy for contemporary political thought.

Rexroth, Kenneth. "The Dialectic of Agony." *Nation*, 12 January 1957, pp. 42–43. Very harsh review of *Notebooks*.

Sontag, Susan. "Simone Weil." In *Against Interpretation and Other Essays*. London: Eyre & Spottiswood, 1967, pp. 49–51. Examines the question why contemporary liberal bourgeois civilization admires the life and work of a figure like Weil.

Taylor, Mark. "History, Humanism and Simone Weil." *Commonweal*, 24 August 1973, pp. 448–52. Written on thirtieth anniversary of Weil's death.

Index

135